SAT I

by
Jerry Bobrow, Ph.D.

Contributing authors
Allan Casson, Ph.D.
Rajiv Rimal, Ph.D.
Jean Eggenschwiler, M.A.

Consultants
Don Gallaher, M.S.
Robert DiPietro, M.A.

IDG
BOOKS
WORLDWIDE

IDG Books Worldwide, Inc.
An International Data Group Company

Foster City, CA ♦ Chicago, IL ♦ Indianapolis, IN ♦ New York, NY

Acknowledgments

I would like to thank Michele Spence of Cliffs Notes for her outstanding editing and careful attention to the production process. Her assistance in this project was invaluable. I would also like to thank my wife, Susan, daughter, Jennifer (21), and sons, Adam (18) and Jonathan (14), for their moral support, comic relief, and staying out of my hair during the writing process (the last item was especially easy for Jennifer, since she was out of the country for the semester).

Finally, I would like to thank the following authors and publishing companies for the use of excerpts from their fine works:

Lucy's Child: The Discovery of a Human Ancestor by Donald Johanson and James Shreeve. Copyright 1989. Reprinted by permission of William Morrow and Co., Inc.

The Constitution: A Documentary and Narrative History by Page Smith. Copyright 1980. Reprinted by permission of William Morrow and Co., Inc.

In Praise of Idleness by Bertrand Russell. Copyright 1962. Reprinted by permission of Unwin Books, George Allen & Unwin, Ltd., Ruskin House.

Women Artists by Ann Sutherland Harris and Linda Nochlin. Copyright 1976. Reprinted by permission of Alfred A. Knopf, Inc.

"The Coming Climate" by Thomas R. Karl, Neville Nicholls, and Jonathan Gregory. Copyright 1997. Reprinted by permission of the authors. Includes British Crown copyright.

Cover photograph by Jean F. Podevin/Image Bank

FIRST EDITION

is a trademark under exclusive license to IDG Books Worldwide, Inc., from International Data Group, Inc.

Your SAT I score can make the difference!
in the college or university you attend.

***Cliffs Quick Review SAT I* can make the difference!**
in the score you get.

So don't take a chance—take an advantage. *Cliffs Quick Review SAT I* was written by leading experts in the field of test preparation, experts who have administered graduate, college entrance, and teacher credentialing test preparation programs for most of the California State Universities for over twenty years. Get the advantage of their expertise and the insights they give you by following this six-step approach:

- **Be aware.** Know as much as you possibly can about the exam before you walk in. This Cliffs Quick Review gives you this important information in a clear and easy-to-understand way.

- **Set a goal.** Call some of the schools you're interested in and see what score you need to be accepted there. This Cliffs Quick Review includes easy-to-use charts to help you set your goal.

- **Know the basic skills.** This Cliffs Quick Review will help you focus on which skills to review and will help you review those skills with practice questions and easy-to-follow, complete explanations.

- **Understand the question types.** This Cliffs Quick Review carefully analyzes each type of question so that you'll understand how to focus on what is being asked.

- **Learn strategies.** This Cliffs Quick Review emphasizes strategies and techniques for answering each type of question and includes samples that show you what to look for and how to apply each strategy.

- **Practice.** This Cliffs Quick Review includes a practice exam with answers, complete explanations, and analysis charts to help you spot your strengths and weaknesses.

Because your study time is valuable, you need this clear, effective, and easy-to-use guide to give you maximum benefit in a reasonable time. Using *Cliffs Quick Review SAT I* and studying regularly will give you the edge in doing your best!

CONTENTS

INTRODUCTION

THE BASICS, THE QUESTIONS, AND THE KEY STRATEGIES FOR VERBAL REASONING

CONTENTS

CONTENTS

THE BASICS, THE QUESTIONS, AND THE KEY STRATEGIES FOR MATHEMATICAL REASONING

CONTENTS

CONTENTS

CONTENTS

PRACTICE TEST

CONTENTS

SCORING AND COMPLETE ANSWERS AND EXPLANATIONS FOR THE PRACTICE TEST

INTRODUCTION

Following are a circle graph and a chart showing the format commonly seen on the SAT I. The actual SAT I is copyrighted and may not be duplicated; and these questions are not taken directly from the acutal tests. **But note these important points.**

- The **order** in which the sections appear and the **number of questions may vary.**

- Only **three of the verbal sections**—two 30-minute sections and one 15-minute section (which generally total 78 questions)—and **three of the math sections**—two 30-minute sections and one 15-minute section (which generally total 60 questions)—**actually count toward your SAT I score.**

- **One 30-minute section is a "pretest," or "experimental," section that does not count toward your score.** This section can be a verbal or a math section and can appear **anywhere** on your exam. It does **not** have to be section 7. **Work all of the sections as though they count toward your score.**

Exam sections and time allotments

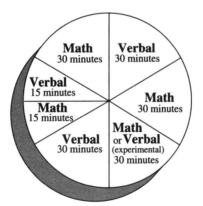

Commonly seen arrangement of sections, time allotments, and number of questions

COMMON FORMAT OF THE SAT I		
(order of sections may vary)		
Section 1 30 minutes	**Mathematical Reasoning** multiple choice	**25 Questions** 25 questions
Section 2 30 minutes	**Verbal Reasoning** sentence completion analogies critical reading (2 passages)	**30 Questions** 9 questions 6 questions 15 questions
Section 3 30 minutes	**Mathematical Reasoning** quantitative comparison grid-ins	**25 Questions** 15 questions 10 questions
Section 4 30 minutes	**Verbal Reasoning** sentence completion analogies critical reading (usually 1 passage)	**35 Questions** 10 questions 13 questions 12 questions
Section 5 15 minutes	**Mathematical Reasoning** multiple choice	**10 Questions** 10 questions
Section 6 15 minutes	**Verbal Reasoning** critical reading (usually paired passages)	**13 Questions** 13 questions
Section 7 30 minutes	**Verbal or Math**	**25-35 Questions**
Total testing time 180 minutes = 3 hours		Approximately 163-173 questions

Who administers the SAT I?

The SAT I is part of the entire Admissions Testing Program (ATP), which is administered by the College Entrance Examination Board in conjunction with Educational Testing Service of Princeton, New Jersey.

Is there a difference between the SAT I and the SAT II?

Yes. The SAT I assesses general verbal and mathematical reading and reasoning abilities that you have developed over your lifetime. The SAT II measures your proficiency in specific subject areas. The SAT II tests how well you have mastered a variety of high school subjects.

Can I take the SAT I more than once?

Yes. But be aware that ATP score reporting is cumulative. That is, your score report will include scores from up to five previous test dates. It isn't uncommon for students to take the test more than once.

What materials may I bring to the SAT I?

Bring your registration form, positive identification, a watch, three or four sharpened Number 2 pencils, a good eraser, and your calculator. You may *not* bring scratch paper or books. You may do your figuring in the margins of the test booklet or in the space provided.

If necessary, may I cancel my score?

Yes. You may cancel your score on the day of the test by telling the test center supervisor, or you may write, fax, or e-mail a cancellation to College Board ATP. Your score report will record your cancellation, along with any completed test scores.

Should I guess on the SAT I?

If you can eliminate one or more of the multiple-choice answers to a question, it is to your advantage to guess. Eliminating one or more answers increases your chance of choosing the right answer. To discourage wild guessing, a fraction of a point is subtracted for every wrong answer, but no points are subtracted if you leave the answer blank. On the grid-in questions, there is no penalty for filling in a wrong answer.

How should I prepare for the SAT I?

Understanding and practicing test-taking strategies will help a great deal, especially on the verbal sections. Subject-matter review is particularly useful for the math sections.

When is the SAT I administered?

Your local college testing or placement office will have information about local administrations; ask for the *Registration Bulletin.* The SAT I is administered at hundreds of schools in and out of the United States.

How and when should I register?

There are two ways to register.

By mail: A registration packet, complete with return envelope, is attached to the *Registration Bulletin.* Mailing in these forms with the appropriate fees completes the registration process.

Online: Simply compete the registration form provided on College Board Online at http://www.collegeboard.org. A Visa, MasterCard, or American Express credit card is required.

How can I reregister?

Those who have previously registered for an SAT Program test can **reregister** by mail, online, or by telephone to take a test again or to take a different test (SAT II). You can call Automated Services at 1-800-728-7267 anytime—twenty-four hours a day, seven days a week (a touch-tone phone and a Visa, MasterCard, or American Express credit card is required). Be sure to get your registration number before you hang up.

Is walk-in registration provided?

Yes, on a limited basis. If you're unable to meet regular registration deadlines, you may attempt to register on the day of the test. (An additional fee is required.) You will be admitted only if space remains after preregistered students have been seated.

When do I get my scores?

You'll usually get your scores within three to four weeks of the test date. You can also use Automated Services (1-800-728-7267) to get your score by phone approximately two weeks after the test date. The fee is about $8 for this service.

Are there testing accommodations for students with disabilities?

Yes. The College Board does make accommodations for students with documented disabilities. If you need accommodations, you should contact the College Board for proper procedures and additional information.

Can I get more information?

Yes. If you require information not available in this book or in the *Registration Bulletin,* you can visit the College Board's World Wide Web site at http://www.collegeboard.org or get SAT Program information at

http://www.collegeboard.org/sat/html/students/indx001.html

You can also write to one of these College Board regional offices:

Middle States:
Suite 410, 3440 Market Street, Philadelphia, Pennsylvania 19104-3338. (215) 387-7600. Fax (215) 387-5805.
or
126 South Swan Street, Albany, New York 12210. (518) 472-1515. Fax (518) 472-1544.

Midwest:
1800 Sherman Avenue, Suite 401, Evanston, Illinois 60201-3715. (708) 866-1700. Fax (708) 866-9280.

New England:
470 Totten Pond Road, Waltham, Massachusetts 02154-1982. (617) 890-9150. Fax (617) 890-0693.

South:
2970 Clairmont Road, Suite 250, Atlanta, Georgia 30329-1639. (404) 636-9465. Fax (404) 633-3006.

Southwest:
701 Brazos Street, Suite 400, Austin, Texas 78701-3253. (512) 472-0231. Fax (512) 472-1401.

West:
2099 Gateway Place, Suite 480, San Jose, California 95110-1017. (408) 452-1400. Fax (408) 453-7396.
or
4155 East Jewell Avenue, Suite 900, Denver, Colorado 80222-4510. (303) 759-1800. Fax (303) 756-8248.
or
Capitol Place, Suite 1200, 915 L Street, Sacramento, California 95814-3700. (916) 444-6262. Fax (916) 444-2868.

Key Strategies for a Positive Approach to the Exam

The key to doing well on the SAT I is to use these positive, active strategies both in your preparation and when you take the exam.

- Set a goal.
- Review basic skills necessary.
- Know the directions.
- Look for winners.

- Don't get stuck.

- Eliminate.

- If you don't know the answer, but can eliminate, guess.

- Don't misread.

- Use a multiple-multiple-choice technique.

- Practice, practice, practice.

- Erase extra marks on your answer sheet.

Set a goal. Contact the colleges or universities you're interested in attending and find out the scores you'll need to get in. (The *Official College Handbook,* published by the College Board, can also give you this valuable information.) Once you've reviewed the scores necessary or the average scores for the schools, then set your personal goals. The following chart, showing the *approximate* number of questions you need to get right to achieve a particular score, will help you do that. In these charts, **check the scores you wish to work toward.**

Verbal Reasoning

	Score	Approximate % right
	800	97% - 100%
	750	92% - 95%
	700	87% - 90%
	650	79% - 82%
	600	69% - 72%
	550	57% - 59%
	500	46% - 49%
	450	34% - 37%
	400	24% - 28%

Mathematical Reasoning

	Score	Approximate % right
	800	99% - 100%
	750	95% - 96%
	700	89% - 91%
	650	80% - 82%
	600	70% - 73%
	550	60% - 62%
	500	49% - 51%
	450	35% - 37%
	400	24% - 25%

$$\begin{aligned} &\textbf{your verbal score goal } \underline{\hspace{1cm}} \\ + \ &\textbf{your math score goal } \underline{\hspace{1cm}} \\ = \ &\textbf{your total score goal } \underline{\hspace{1cm}} \end{aligned}$$

Review basic skills necessary. As you begin your preparation, you should review the basic skills you need to do well. For the math sections, a quick review of basic arithmetic, algebra I, and intuitive geometry will give you a good foundation. For the verbal sections, reviewing common prefixes, suffixes, and roots and working on reading comprehension skills will be helpful. Remember, the best way to build reading skills and a good vocabulary is to read (a lot). A short method to help improve some reading skills is to quickly read an article from a magazine and then summarize the main point of the article in one sentence. To make this method most effective, write out each sentence and repeat the exercise with at least four or five articles.

Know the directions. The SAT I is composed of six types of questions: multiple-choice math, quantitative comparison, grid-ins, analogies, sentence completion, and critical reading. Read and review the directions for each of these types of questions carefully before the day of the test so that you'll be completely familiar with them.

Look for winners. Go into each test section looking for questions you can answer and should get right. Keep in mind which types of problems are in order of difficulty so you'll know where the easy, average, and difficult questions are located. Each group of test questions is ordered in this way *except* critical reading questions. Critical reading questions are *not* arranged in any such order, so a difficult reading question can be followed by an easy one. Remember, *the basis for a good score is getting the questions right that you can and should get right.*

Don't get stuck. Since each question within a section is worth the same amount, you should never get stuck on any one question. Using the following marking system on your answer sheet can help.

1. Answer easy questions immediately.

2. Place a + (plus) next to any problem that seems solvable but is too time consuming.

3. Place a – (minus) next to any question that seems impossible. Act quickly; don't waste time deciding whether a question is a plus or a minus.

After answering all the questions you can immediately answer, go back and work on your + questions. If you finish them, try your – questions (sometimes when you come back to a question that seemed impossible, you'll suddenly realize how to answer it). Your answer sheet should look something like this after you finish answering your easy questions.

1. Ⓐ ● Ⓒ Ⓓ Ⓔ
+2. Ⓐ Ⓑ Ⓒ Ⓓ Ⓔ
3. Ⓐ Ⓑ ● Ⓓ Ⓔ
– 4. Ⓐ Ⓑ Ⓒ Ⓓ Ⓔ
+5. Ⓐ Ⓑ Ⓒ Ⓓ Ⓔ

Make sure to erase your + and – marks before your time is up.
The scoring machine may count extraneous marks as wrong answers.

Knowing when to skip a question is invaluable. Because, as mentioned, each question in a section is of equal value, don't spend more than a minute or a minute and a half on any one question. The only exception to this timing is if you've set a goal that doesn't require you to get the more difficult questions right. In that case, on any section in which the questions are in order of difficulty, you could spend a little more time on the easy and average questions.

Eliminate. As soon as you know that an answer choice is wrong, eliminate it. As you eliminate an answer choice from consideration, take advantage of being allowed to mark in your testing booklet by marking out the eliminated answer in your question booklet as follows:

$$(\cancel{A})$$
$$? \ (B)$$
$$(\cancel{C})$$
$$(\cancel{D})$$
$$? \ (E)$$

Notice that some choices are marked with question marks, signifying that they may be possible answers. This technique will help you avoid reconsidering those choices you've already eliminated and will help you narrow down your possible answers. *These marks in your testing booklet do not need to be erased.*

If you don't know the answer, but can eliminate, guess. Since there's a penalty for guessing on most questions on the SAT I, *you should guess only if you can eliminate one or more choices.* Keep in mind that you can often eliminate ridiculous or unreasonable answers. *But remember, don't guess blindly.* The math grid-in questions are the only ones in which there is no penalty for guessing. On these questions, guess if you need to.

Don't misread. One of the most common mistakes on most exams is misreading the question. You must be sure you know what the question is asking. For example,

1.

   Notice that this question doesn't ask for the value of x, but rather the value of

Or

2. All of the following statements could be true EXCEPT . . .

Or

3. Which of the following is NOT a possible explanation . . .?

   Notice that the words EXCEPT and NOT change these questions significantly.

To avoid misreading a question (and therefore answering it incorrectly), simply *underline or circle* what you must answer in the question. For example, do you have to find x or $x + 3$. Are you looking for what could be true or the *exception* to what could be true? To help in avoiding misreads, mark the questions in your booklet in this way.

1. If $4x + 6 = 26$, what is the value of $x + 3$?

2. All of the following statements <u>could</u> be <u>true EXCEPT</u> . . .

3. Which of the following is <u>NOT</u> a <u>possible explanation</u> . . .?

*Remember that these underlines or circles in your **question booklet** do **not** have to be erased.*

Use a multiple-multiple-choice technique. Some math and verbal questions use a "multiple-multiple-choice" format. At first glance, these questions appear more confusing and more difficult than normal five-choice (A, B, C, D, E) multiple-choice questions. Actually, once you understand "multiple-multiple-choice" question types and the techniques you can use to answer them, they are often easier than comparable multiple-choice questions. For example,

1. If x is a positive integer, then which of the following must be true?

    I. $x > 0$
    II. $x = 0$
    III. $x < 1$

    (A) I only
    (B) II only
    (C) III only
    (D) I and II only
    (E) I and III only

Since x is a positive integer, it must be a counting number. Note that possible values of x could be 1, or 2, or 3, or 4, and so on. Therefore, statement I, $x > 0$, is always true. So next to I on your question booklet, place a T for *true*.

$$\mathsf{T} \quad \begin{array}{l} \text{I.}\quad x > 0 \\ \text{II.}\quad x = 0 \\ \text{III.}\quad x < 1 \end{array}$$

Now realize that the correct final answer choice (A, B, C, D, or E) *must* contain *true statement I*. This eliminates (B) and (C) as possible correct answer choices, as they do *not* contain true statement I. You should cross out (B) and (C) on your question booklet.

Statement II is *incorrect.* If x is positive, x cannot equal zero. Thus, next to II, you should place an F for *false.*

$$
\begin{array}{ll}
\text{T} & \text{I. } x > 0 \\
\text{F} & \text{II. } x = 0 \\
& \text{III. } x < 1
\end{array}
$$

Knowing that II is false allows you to eliminate any answer choices that contain *false statement II.* Therefore, you should cross out (D), as it contains false statement II. Only (A) and (E) are left as possible correct answers.

Finally, you realize that statement III is also false, as x must be 1 or greater. So you place an F next to III, thus eliminating choice (E) and leaving (A), I only. This technique often saves some precious time and allows you to take a better educated guess should you not be able to complete all parts (I, II, and III) of a multiple-multiple-choice question.

Practice, practice, practice. Nothing beats practice. You can't practice too much. But the important thing in practicing is to learn from your mistakes, so it's important that you go back and carefully analyze and correct your mistakes. Analyzing and correcting will help you focus your review and eliminate your common mistakes. When you practice, try to simulate the testing conditions—that is, no scratch paper, a small desk, no books, including dictionaries, and so forth. The only difference between your practice and the real thing is that when you practice, you should short yourself slightly on time. Instead of giving yourself 30 minutes on a section, for example, give yourself 25 or 27 minutes, which will help you work at a good pace.

Erase extra marks on your answer sheet. Because the scoring machine may count extra marks on the answer sheet as wrong answers, be sure to erase any you've put there before time is up.

THE BASICS, THE QUESTIONS, AND THE KEY
STRATEGIES FOR VERBAL REASONING

The Skills You'll Use

The Verbal Reasoning sections test your ability

- to understand logical relationships between pairs of words

- to complete sentences with a word or words that retain the meaning and structure of the sentence

- to understand, interpret, and analyze reading passages on a variety of topics

The Types of Questions

Verbal Reasoning consists of three basic types of questions.

- analogies

- sentence completion questions

- critical reading questions

About half of the Verbal Reasoning questions are critical reading questions.

Your Verbal Reasoning Score

Three Verbal Reasoning sections count toward your score: a 30-minute section that contains about 30 questions (generally 9 sentence completion questions, 6 analogies, and two critical reading passages with about 15 total questions), another 30-minute section that contains about 35 questions (generally 10 sentence completion questions,

13 analogies, and usually one critical reading passage with about 12 questions), and finally a 15-minute section that contains 12 to 15 critical reading questions usually based on two related (paired) passages. Some questions concern one passage or the other, and some concern both passages. *Paired passages can also appear in a 30-minute section.*

Although the order of the sections and the number of questions may change, at this time, the three sections total about 78 questions that count toward your score. A scaled verbal score from 200 to 800 is generated by these three verbal sections (78 questions). About 50% right should generate an average score (approximately 500).

Verbal Reasoning

(approximately 78 questions
that count toward your score)

The Levels of Difficulty

The questions within each of the sentence completion and analogy sections are arranged in slight graduation of difficulty from easier to more demanding questions (often based on the difficulty of the words used). Basically, the first few questions are the easiest; the middle few are of average difficulty; and the last few are difficult. *There is no such pattern for the critical reading passages or questions.*

Some Help to Get You Started

Common prefixes, suffixes, and roots. The following list should help you get started in arriving at definitions of unfamiliar words on the Verbal Reasoning section. These and other prefixes, suffixes, and roots apply to thousands of words.

Prefixes

Prefix	*Meaning*	*Example*
ad-	to, toward	advance
anti-	against	antidote
bi-	two	bicycle
com-	together, with	composite
de-	away, from	deter
epi-	upon	epicenter
equi-	equal, equally	equivalent
ex-	out of	expel
homo-	same, equal, like	homogenized
hyper-	over, too much	hyperactive
hypo-	under, too little	hypodermic
in-	into	instruct
in-	not	insufficient
inter-	between	interstate
mal-	bad	malfunction
mis-	wrong	mistake
mono-	alone, one	monolith
non-	not	nonentity
ob-	against	objection
omni-	all, everywhere	omniscient
over-	above	overbearing
poly-	many	polymorphous
pre-	before	precede
pro-	forward	propel
re-	back, again	regress

retro-	backward	retrograde
semi-	half, partly	semicircle
sub-	under	submarine
trans-	across, beyond	transcend
un-	not	unneeded

Suffixes

Suffix	*Meaning*	*Example*
-able, -ible	able to	usable
-er, -or	one who does	competitor
-fy	to make	dignify
-ism	the practice of	rationalism
-ist	one who is occupied with	feminist
-less	without, lacking	meaningless
-logue	a particular kind of speaking or writing	prologue
-ness	the quality of	aggressiveness
-ship	the condition of, skill of	partisanship
-tude	the state of	rectitude

Roots

Root	*Meaning*	*Example*
arch	to rule	monarch
belli	war, warlike	belligerent
bene	good	benevolent
chron	time	chronology
dic	to say	indicative
fac	to make, to do	artifact
graph	writing	telegraph
mort	to die	mortal
port	to carry	deport
vid, vis	to see	invisible

The Basics of Analogy Questions

The number of questions. You will have from about 6 to about 13 analogies on each of two verbal sections of your exam, for a total of about 19 questions. Remember, in each section, the analogy questions are *generally* arranged in order from easier to more difficult.

The directions. In each question, you're given a related pair of words or phrases. Select the lettered pair that *best* expresses a relationship similar to that in the original pair.

The Questions and Key Strategies for Analogy Questions

- Know how the words are being used.
- Construct a sentence relating the two words.
- Make the sentence as specific as possible.
- Note the order of the words.
- Consider the secondary relationship.
- Watch the "level" of each word.
- Realize that the sets of words don't have to be in the same category.

Know how the words are being used. First make sure you know what both words in the first pair mean. Note that a word may have many meanings, often depending on how it is used or its part of

speech. The word *hand,* for example, can be a noun (referring to the grasping part at the end of your arm or to applause, as in "Give the performers a *hand)* or a verb (referring to the action of giving something, as in "Hand the ball to me").

To determine what the parts of speech in the original are, look at the five answer choices. All of them will be the same parts of speech as those in the original pair. So if you're not sure about a word in the first pair, the words in the choices will tell you what parts of speech are being used.

Sample:

1. PARK : CITY ::
   (A) oasis : desert
   (B) book : store
   (C) water : waterfall
   (D) fence : home
   (E) chair : furniture

The word *park* may be a verb meaning to leave a vehicle in a certain location or a noun describing land set aside in a *city* for rest or recreation. The answer choices make clear that *park* is a noun here. The best choice is (A). The relationship between *park* and *city* is the same as the relationship between *oasis* and *desert.*

Construct a sentence relating the two words. To help determine the relationship between the words in the original pair, construct a sentence using the words that explains how the two words are related. Then use almost the same sentence, replacing the original words with the answer choices.

Sample:

2. RECIPE : COOKBOOK ::
   (A) letter : stamp
   (B) formula : chemist
   (C) blueprint : building
   (D) map : atlas
   (E) prescription : pharmacy

   The best answer is (D). A sentence you could use is "A *recipe* is found in a *cookbook*." You could then try each of the choices. (A) A *letter* is found in a *stamp*. NO. (B) A *formula* is found in a *chemist*. NO. (C) A *blueprint* is found in a *building*. Possibly, but not usually. (D) A *map* is found in an *atlas*. Absolutely! (E) A *prescription* is found in a *pharmacy*. Possibly, but not necessarily. Perhaps better sentences are "A *recipe* is contained in a *cookbook*" and "A *map* is contained in an *atlas*."

   Notice how constructing a sentence relating the two words can be very helpful in solving an analogy. The actual analogy can be stated as follows: "*Recipe* is to *cookbook* in the same way as *map* is to *atlas*." The standard analogy sentence is "A is to B in the same way as C is to D."

Make the sentence as specific as possible. Since some of the choices may be generally the same, make your sentence as precise as you can. If your sentence isn't specific, a few answer choices may seem good.

Sample:

3. HAND : MAN ::
   (A) tail : dog
   (B) paw : cat
   (C) bumper : car
   (D) rain : umbrella
   (E) head : hat

The best choice is (B). Using the sentence "A *hand* is a part of a *man*" will eliminate choices (D) and (E), but it isn't specific enough to get the right answer. Choice (A) "A *tail* is a part of a *dog*," choice (B) "A *paw* is a part of a *cat*," and choice (C) "A *bumper* is a part of a *car*" are all possibilities with this general sentence. But if you make the sentence more specific, such as "A *hand* is a part of a *man* that is used for grasping," then choices (A) and (C) can be eliminated. Remember that making a clear and specific sentence showing the relationship between the first two words will usually eliminate wrong answers and lead you to the best choice.

Note the order of the words. Be sure to keep the order of your answer pair like the order of the first pair. Wrong answers may present a correct relationship but in the wrong order.

Sample:

4. HEADACHE : ASPIRIN ::
   (A) insect : insecticide
   (B) allergy : ragweed
   (C) quinine : malaria
   (D) infection : antibiotic
   (E) poison : toxin

The best choice is (D). As a *headache* may be cured by an *aspirin,* an *infection* may be cured by an *antibiotic.* Although *quinine* is taken to prevent or reduce the symptoms of *malaria,* the order of the two terms here reverses that of the original pair. Remember that maintaining the order given in your original sentence, "A *headache* may be cured by an *aspirin,*" is key.

Keep the sentence order consistent. Sometimes it's easier to make up a sentence using the original words in reverse order. Remember in this case to reverse the order of the words in the choices when you try them in your sentence.

Sample:

5. ARROW : QUIVER ::
   (A) actor : applause
   (B) garage : car
   (C) editorial : newspaper
   (D) pistol : holster
   (E) dirt : shovel

The best choice is (D). "A *quiver* is a case for holding an *arrow.*" The closest parallel is "A *holster* is a case for holding a *pistol.*" Notice that in this situation it is probably easier to make a sentence starting from the second word. Just remember that each of your sentences for this question must then be consistent and start from the second word.

Consider the secondary relationship. You may need to consider not only the primary relationship between the original words but also a secondary relationship.

Sample:

6. FINE : SPEEDING ::
   (A) watch : retiring
   (B) certificate : achieving
   (C) key : unlocking
   (D) payment : working
   (E) penalty : fouling

The best choice is (E). "*Speeding* can cause you to get a *fine.*" This sentence tells you that the original relationship is between an action and a result of that action. The primary relationship is that the second word, the action, results in getting the thing indicated by the first word. Choices (A) "*Retiring* can cause you to get a *watch,*" (B) "*Achieving* can cause you to get a *certificate,*" and (D) "*Working* can cause you to get a *payment*" all indicate actions (second word) that could cause one to get the thing indicated by the first word. But the secondary relationship is that *speeding* is **illegal** and is **punishable** by a *fine.* This secondary relationship helps you focus on the important specifics needed for the right answer. Choice (E) reflects both the primary and the secondary relationships. "*Fouling* can cause you to get a *penalty,*" and "*Fouling* is illegal by the governing rules and is punishable by a *penalty.*"

Watch the "level" of each word. Carefully examine each word, especially if you have trouble with the meaning, and note the "level" of the word. Is the word extreme, harsh, soft, or gentle?

Sample:

7. LOUD : BLARING ::
   - (A) impotent : potent
   - (B) tepid : warm
   - (C) surprising : shocking
   - (D) cool : calm
   - (E) noise : quiet

   The best choice is (C). Say that you don't know the meaning of the term *blaring,* but you do recall hearing it used very negatively. So you could assume that it is a harsh or extreme word. The only second word that is harsh or extreme is *shocking.* *Blaring* is the extreme of *loud* in the same way as *shocking* is the extreme of *surprising.* So if you don't know the relationship between the original words, or even the meaning of the words, you can sometimes get the right answer by using this strategy to make an educated guess.

Realize that the sets of words don't have to be in the same category. Remember that your choice, the second set of words, doesn't have to come from the same category, class, or type as do the original words. You're looking for words that have the same *relationship*.

Sample:

8. TASTING : EATING ::
   (A) skimming : reading
   (B) cooking : cleaning
   (C) singing : dining
   (D) baking : broiling
   (E) laughing : smiling

The best choice is (A). Notice that the original words, *tasting* and *eating,* are from the universe or category of food, and notice that three of the choices, (B), (C), and (D), have words from the same category. But you're looking for the words that have the same *relationship* as the original pair, not words from the same category. *Tasting* is *eating* or drinking in small quantities, lightly. *Skimming* is *reading* in small quantities, lightly, swiftly. Even though *skimming* and *reading* are from the universe or category of written material, not food, this pair has the closest relationship to the original pair and is the best answer.

The Basics of Sentence Completion Questions

The number of questions. You will have about 9 or 10 sentence completion questions on each of two verbal sections of your exam, for a total of about 19 questions. Remember, in each section, the sentence completion questions are *generally* arranged in order from easier to more difficult.

The directions. Each blank in the following sentences indicates that something has been omitted. Consider the lettered words beneath the sentence and choose the word or set of words that best fits the whole sentence.

The Questions and Key Strategies for Sentence Completion Questions

- Think of words you would insert as answers.
- Look for signal words connecting contrasting ideas.
- Notice signal words connecting similar ideas.
- Focus on signal words that help define words.
- Watch for contrasts between positive and negative.
- Be aware of the direction of the sentence.
- Attempt questions one word at a time.
- Work from the second word first.
- Read in each choice.

Think of words you would insert as answers. *After* reading the sentence and *before* looking at the answer choices, think of words you would insert and then look for synonyms of them in the answer choices.

Sample:

1. Altlhough it was not apparent at the time, in ---- we can see how Miles Davis's performances in the 1970s were ---- by what was happening then in popular music.
   (A) retrospect . . influenced
   (B) effect . . modified
   (C) fact . . unchanged
   (D) foresight . . endangered
   (E) time . . engendered

The best choice is (A). After reading the sentence, you may decide that the phrase *not apparent at the time* would suggest *looking back* for the first blank and that the second word needs to be *affected.* You could read the sentence "Although it was not apparent at the time, in *looking back* we can see how Miles Davis's performances in the 1970s were *affected* by what was happening then in popular music." Now, looking for synonyms for *looking back* and *affected* gives you choice (A) *retrospect . . influenced.*

Look for signal words connecting contrasting ideas. Spotting signal words in the sentence can be invaluable. Some signal words, such as *however, although, on the other hand, but, instead, despite, regardless, rather, than,* and *except,* connect contrasting ideas.

Sample:

2. Surfing was once a sociable pastime, but now joining another surfer on a wave is ---- as heinous as cutting off another driver on the highway.
   (A) an occasion
   (B) an offense
   (C) an adage
   (D) a discourtesy
   (E) an amenity

The best choice is (B). The first clause of the sentence contrasts a time when surfing was *sociable* with the present, so the last half of the sentence must describe an antisocial action. The word *but* tips off the contrast. Choices (B) *an offense* and (D) *a discourtesy* are the only two that contrast with *sociable*. *An offense* is the better choice, since *a discourtesy* is not strong enough to fit well with *heinous* (shockingly evil).

Notice signal words connecting similar ideas. Other signal words, such as *in other words, besides, and, in addition, also, therefore, furthermore,* and *as,* often connect similar ideas.

Sample:

3. We need experiments to discover if the systems that we have designed that work in theory also work in ----, in other words, in the real world.
   (A) hypotheses
   (B) fact
   (C) space
   (D) part
   (E) essence

The best choice is (B). The key words here are *in other words,* which tell you that your choice must be similar to *the real world.* The terms *in fact* and *in the real world* both refer to similar ideas in this sentence.

Focus on signal words that help define words. Still other signal words will actually give you a definition or point you to the definition of the word needed.

Sample:

4. The unique world of the film is ----, both wholly recognizable and unfamiliar.
   (A) contradictory
   (B) realistic
   (C) simplistic
   (D) timeless
   (E) unchanging

   The best choice is (A). The second part of this sentence, *both wholly recognizable and unfamiliar,* is a perfect example of the word needed, *contradictory.* The words *recognizable* and *unfamiliar* **contradict** each other (are opposite).

Watch for contrasts between positive and negative. As you read the sentence, watch for contrasts between positive or negative. Such contrasts are often signaled by such words as *not, never,* and *no.*

Sample:

5. Malcolm did not ---- the filmed version of his novel but rather
   ---- it because all of the exciting parts that he had written were
   excluded.
   (A) love .. liked
   (B) appreciate .. was appalled by
   (C) hate .. detested
   (D) approve .. accepted
   (E) dismiss .. applauded

   The best choice is (B). The word *not* indicates that the first blank
   must be the opposite of the second blank. Choices (A), (C), and
   (D) do not give opposites. Choices (B) and (E) could both be seen
   as opposites, but only choice (B) makes sense in the sentence. If
   all of the exciting parts of the novel were left out, it's reasonable
   to assume that the author would *not* like (*appreciate*) that fact.

Be aware of the direction of the sentence. Negative words can
change the direction of the sentence, sometimes making the logic of
the sentence more difficult to follow.

Sample:

6. The room was in an advanced state of disrepair; not only were
   the velvet draperies ----, but they were also mottled and ----.
   (A) bright .. torn
   (B) old .. clean
   (C) faded .. frayed
   (D) new .. mangled
   (E) tattered .. original

The best choice is (C). The logic of this sentence could be diffi-cult to follow because of the negative wording. *State of disrepair* tips you off that both blanks must be filled with negative words. Choice (C) *faded . . frayed* is the only negative pair. The words also fit the meaning of the sentence.

Attempt questions one word at a time. Questions with two words missing should be attempted one word at a time. But remember that both words must fit.

Sample:

7. The government ---- that the new laws are necessary to prevent unscrupulous business owners from ---- off the profits while the workers are underpaid.
   (A) implies . . dilating
   (B) anticipates . . privatizing
   (C) infers . . acquiring
   (D) requires . . living
   (E) contends . . siphoning

   The best choice is (E). The only first words that make sense in the sentence are choices (A) *implies,* (B) *anticipates,* and (E) *contends.* But the second word in choice (E), *siphoning,* is the only one that fits. "*Siphoning* off profits" is a common phrase and is something that unscrupulous business owners might try to do.

Work from the second word first. Sometimes it's more efficient to work from the second blank first.

Sample:

8. The program, which ---- housing for disadvantaged **families,** should be a tremendous ---- to the beneficiaries who are **able to** meet income requirements.
   (A) allows . . detriment
   (B) provides . . boon
   (C) insures . . expenditure
   (D) includes . . drawback
   (E) eliminates . . benefit

   The best choice is (B). Since there are many possibilities for the first blank, you may wish to start with the second blank. The phrase *a tremendous ---- to the beneficiaries* tells you that this second blank must be a "positive" word because being a beneficiary (one who benefits) is positive. So you should look for a positive second word and then try the first word. Choices (B) *boon* and (E) *benefit* are the only two answers with second words that fit. Now take each choice and see if the first word also fits. Choice (B) *provides . . boon* (advantage) makes complete sense. Although the second word in choice (E) fits perfectly, the first word doesn't make sense in the sentence. Again, keep in mind that each word must fit for the answer to be correct.

Read in each choice. If you don't spot any signal words or you don't know the meaning of some of the choices (or if you're just stumped), quickly read each answer choice and see which sounds best. Sometimes this last method will help you at least eliminate some of the choices so you can take an educated guess.

Sample:

9. Many lawyers now believe that the ---- of the tobacco industry is so widely ---- by the public that juries will finally be willing to convict the corporations when the cases go to trial.
   (A) advertising . . disseminated
   (B) propaganda . . credited
   (C) repute . . supported
   (D) mendacity . . queried
   (E) guilt . . acknowledged

   The best choice is (E). If you quickly read each choice into the sentence, you'll notice that some of the choices just don't seem to make sense, sound right, or fit. Since the last part of the sentence says *willing to convict the corporations when the cases go to trial,* the idea that the *guilt* is *acknowledged* sounds good and fits perfectly.

A special reminder: Always read your answer into the sentence to make sure it makes sense. Reading in your answer will often help you avoid oversights or simple mistakes.

The Basics of Critical Reading Passages and Questions

The length of passages and number of questions. The critical reading passages range from 400 to 850 words. The shorter passages are followed by 5 to 9 questions, while the longer passages can be followed by 12 to 13 questions. In one section, there are two related, or paired, passages—which total about 750 to 900 words—with 13 to 15 questions following the "double passage." Each exam will contain about 40 critical reading questions, which will account for about 50% of your verbal score.

The passage content. The passages on each exam come from four content areas: humanities, social sciences, natural sciences, and narrative (fiction or nonfiction). These passages are sophisticated and thoughtful discussions dealing with important topics, events, and ideas. Each passage contains numbered lines.

The question types. The majority of the questions require careful thinking and reasoning, not just a basic understanding of the passage. Common types of questions ask you

- about the main idea, main point, purpose, or a possible title of the passage
- about information that is directly stated in the passage
- about information that is assumed, implied, or suggested or that can be inferred
- about the meaning of a word or phrase in a passage
- to recognize applications of the author's opinions or ideas

- to evaluate how the author develops and presents the passage

- to recognize the style or tone of the passage

The directions. Questions follow each of the passages below. Using only the stated or implied information in each passage and in its introduction, if any, answer the questions.

The Questions and Key Strategies for Critical Reading Questions Based on Single Passages

General strategies.

- Read the passage actively, marking the main points and other items you feel are important.

- Pace yourself. Don't get stuck on the passage or any one question.

- Base your answer on the passage, the introduction, or any footnotes.

- Preread a few questions. Prereading can give you a clue about the passage and what to look for.

Specific strategies for questions based on single passages.

- Read the passage looking for its main point and its structure.

- Make sure that your answer is supported by the passage.

- Make sure that the answer you select "answers the question." Some good or true answers are not correct.

- As you read, note the tone of the passage.

- Take advantage of the line numbers.

- Use the context to figure out the meaning of words, even if you're unfamiliar with them.

- Read all the choices, since you're looking for the *best* answer given.

- Use an elimination strategy.

Read the passage actively, marking the main points and other items you feel are important. You can mark a passage by underlining or circling important information. But be sure you don't over-mark, or you'll defeat the purpose of the technique. The following passage shows one way a test taker might mark a passage to assist in understanding the information given and to quickly return to particular information in the passage when necessary. You may find that circling works better for you or using other marks that you personally find helpful.

Sample passage:

Human beings have in recent years discovered that they may have succeeded in achieving a <u>momentous</u> but rather <u>unwanted accomplishment</u>. Because of our numbers and our technology, it now seems likely that we have begun <u>altering</u>

(5) the <u>climate</u> of our planet.

Climatologists are confident that over the past century, the global <u>average temperature</u> has <u>increased</u> about half a degree Celsius. This warming is thought to be at least <u>partly</u> the <u>result of human activity</u>, such as the burning of fossil fuels in power

(10) plants and automobiles. Moreover, because populations, national economies, and the use of technology are all growing, the global average temperature is <u>expected to continue increasing</u>, by an additional 1.0 to 3.5 degrees C by the year 2100.

(15) Such warming is just one of the many consequences that climate change can have. Nevertheless, the ways that

warming might affect the planet's environment—and, therefore, its life—are among the most <u>compelling issues</u> in earth
science. Unfortunately, they are also among the most difficult
(20) to predict. The effects will be complex and vary considerably
from place to place. <u>Of particular interest</u> are the changes in
<u>regional climate</u> and local weather and especially <u>extreme</u>
<u>events</u>—record temperatures, heat waves, very heavy rainfall,
or drought, for example—which could very well have stagger-
(25) ing effects on societies, agriculture, and ecosystems.

   Based on studies of how the earth's weather has changed
over the past century as global temperatures edged upward as
well as on sophisticated computer models of climate, it now
seems probable that warming will accompany <u>changes</u> in
(30) <u>regional weather</u>. For example, longer and more intense heat
waves—a likely consequence of an increase in either the mean
temperature or in the variability of daily temperatures—would
<u>result</u> in public <u>health threats</u> and even unprecedented levels
of <u>mortality</u>, as well as in such costly <u>inconveniences</u> as road
(35) buckling and high cooling loads, the latter possibly leading to
electrical brownouts or blackouts.

   <u>Climate change</u> would also <u>affect</u> the <u>patterns</u> of <u>rainfall</u>
and other precipitation, with some areas getting more and oth-
ers less, changing global patterns and occurrences of droughts
(40) and floods. Similarly, increased variability and extremes in
precipitation can <u>exacerbate existing problems</u> in water quality and sewage treatment and in erosion and urban storm-
water routing, among others. Such possibilities underscore the
<u>need to understand</u> the <u>consequences</u> of humankind's effect
(45) on global climate.

   Researchers have <u>two main</u>—and complementary—
<u>methods of investigating</u> these climate changes. <u>Detailed</u>
<u>meteorological records</u> go back about a century, which coin-
cides with the period during which the global average temper-
(50) ature increased by half a degree. By examining these measurements and records, climatologists are beginning to get a

picture of how and where extremes of weather and climate have occurred.

(55) It is the <u>relation between these extremes</u> and the <u>overall temperature increase</u> that really interests scientists. This is where <u>another critical research tool</u>—global ocean-atmosphere <u>climate models</u>—comes in. These high-performance computer programs simulate the important processes of the atmosphere and oceans, giving researchers insights into the <u>links between</u>
(60) <u>human activities</u> and <u>major weather and climate events</u>.

The <u>combustion</u> of fossil fuels, for example, increases the concentration in the atmosphere of certain <u>greenhouse gases</u>, the fundamental agents of the global warming that may be attributable to humans. These gases, which include carbon
(65) dioxide, methane, ozone, halocarbons, and nitrous oxide, let in sunlight but tend to insulate the planet against the loss of heat, <u>not unlike the glass of a greenhouse</u>. Thus a <u>higher concentration</u> means a <u>warmer climate</u>.

Preread a few questions. Prereading can give you a clue about the passage and what to look for. Quickly reading a few of the questions before reading the passage may be very helpful, especially if the passage seems difficult or unfamiliar to you. *In prereading, read only the questions and NOT the answer choices* (which aren't included in the examples below). Notice that you should mark (underline or circle) what the question is asking. After you read the passage, you'll go on to read the questions again and each of their answer choices. The following questions give examples of ways to mark as you preread.

1. Which of the following would be the <u>best title</u> for this passage?

Notice that *best title* is marked. This is a main-point question and tips you off that you should be sure to read for the main point in the passage.

2. Which of the following <u>inferences</u> is <u>NOT supported</u> by information in the passage?

Notice that *inferences . . . NOT supported* is marked. To answer this question, you'll need to draw information from the passage by "reading between the lines."

3. According to the passage, which of the following terms <u>best describes</u> the <u>effects of global warming</u>?

Notice that *best describes . . . effects of global warming* is marked. You now know that the passage involves the effects of global warming.

4. Which of the following best describes the <u>author's tone</u> in this passage?

The words *author's tone* are marked here. You now know to pay special attention to the tone of the passage.

After such prereading and marking of the questions, you should go back and read the passage actively. The passage is reprinted below without the marking. Try marking it yourself this time before you go on to the sample questions that follow.

Questions 1-8 are based on the following reading passage.

Human beings have in recent years discovered that they may have succeeded in achieving a momentous but rather unwanted accomplishment. Because of our numbers and our technology, it now seems likely that we have begun altering
(5) the climate of our planet.

Climatologists are confident that over the past century, the global average temperature has increased about half a degree Celsius. This warming is thought to be at least partly the result of human activity, such as the burning of fossil fuels in power

(10) plants and automobiles. Moreover, because populations, national economies, and the use of technology are all growing, the global average temperature is expected to continue increasing, by an additional 1.0 to 3.5 degrees C by the year 2100.

(15) Such warming is just one of the many consequences that climate change can have. Nevertheless, the ways that warming might affect the planet's environment—and, therefore, its life—are among the most compelling issues in earth science. Unfortunately, they are also among the most difficult to predict.

(20) The effects will be complex and vary considerably from place to place. Of particular interest are the changes in regional climate and local weather and especially extreme events— record temperatures, heat waves, very heavy rainfall, or drought, for example—which could very well have stagger-

(25) ing effects on societies, agriculture, and ecosystems.

Based on studies of how the earth's weather has changed over the past century as global temperatures edged upward as well as on sophisticated computer models of climate, it now seems probable that warming will accompany changes in

(30) regional weather. For example, longer and more intense heat waves—a likely consequence of an increase in either the mean temperature or in the variability of daily temperatures—would result in public health threats and even unprecedented levels of mortality, as well as in such costly inconveniences as road

(35) buckling and high cooling loads, the latter possibly leading to electrical brownouts or blackouts.

Climate change would also affect the patterns of rainfall and other precipitation, with some areas getting more and others less, changing global patterns and occurrences of droughts

(40) and floods. Similarly, increased variability and extremes in

precipitation can exacerbate existing problems in water quality and sewage treatment and in erosion and urban storm-
water routing, among others. Such possibilities underscore the
need to understand the consequences of humankind's effect
(45)   on global climate.

Researchers have two main—and complementary—
methods of investigating these climate changes. Detailed
meteorological records go back about a century, which
coincides with the period during which the global average
(50)   temperature increased by half a degree. By examining these
measurements and records, climatologists are beginning to get
a picture of how and where extremes of weather and climate
have occurred.

It is the relation between these extremes and the overall tem-
(55)   perature increase that really interests scientists. This is where
another critical research tool—global ocean-atmosphere climate models—comes in. These high-performance computer
programs simulate the important processes of the atmosphere
and oceans, giving researchers insights into the links between
(60)   human activities and major weather and climate events.

The combustion of fossil fuels, for example, increases the
concentration in the atmosphere of certain greenhouse gases,
the fundamental agents of the global warming that may be
attributable to humans. These gases, which include carbon
(65)   dioxide, methane, ozone, halocarbons, and nitrous oxide, let
in sunlight but tend to insulate the planet against the loss of
heat, not unlike the glass of a greenhouse. Thus a higher concentration means a warmer climate.

Read the passage looking for its main point and structure. As you read the passage, try to focus on "what the author is really saying" or "what point the author is trying to make." There are many ways to ask about the main point of a passage.

Sample:

1. Which of the following would be the best title for this passage?
   (A) The History of Climate
   (B) Fossil Fuels and Greenhouse Gases
   (C) Extremes of Climate
   (D) Global Warming and the Changing Climate
   (E) Methods of Researching Global Climate

   The best choice is (D). Asking for the *best title* is a main-point, or main-idea, type question. Now take a careful look at each answer choice. Choice (A) is too broad; also, the passage doesn't actually deal with the *history* of climate. Choices (B), (C), and (E), on the other hand, are too narrow. While it's true that all of these topics are touched upon in the passage, a title should cover the passage as a whole.

Make sure that your answer is supported by the passage. Every single correct answer is in the passage or can be directly inferred from the passage.

Sample:

2. Which of the following inferences is NOT supported by information in the passage?

 (A) Computer models of climate have proved superior to old meteorological records in helping climatologists pinpoint changes.

 (B) Changes in climate are affected by both natural and human activities.

 (C) Whatever the changes that occur in North America's climate over the next two hundred years, it is unlikely they will be accompanied by cooler average temperatures.

 (D) Dramatic changes in precipitation could have negative effects, producing both droughts and floods.

 (E) Increased industrialization in developing countries could lead to increases in the rate of global warming.

The best choice is (A). This is a tricky question, since it asks you which of the answer choices is NOT supported by the passage. The author mentions two ways of researching climate changes but describes them as *complementary,* not as superior or inferior. Therefore, choice (A) is NOT supported by the passage. You might be tempted by choice (B), but notice that lines 8-10 state that warming is thought to be at least *partly* the result of human activity, suggesting that natural forces are involved as well. Choice (C) is supported in lines 28-30, choice (D) in lines 37-43, and choice (E) in lines 10-14.

Make sure that the answer you select "answers the question." Some good or true answers are not correct. Even though more than one choice may be true, you're looking for the *best* answer to the question given.

Sample:

3. According to the passage, which of the following terms best describes the effects of global warming?
   (A) Complex
   (B) Disastrous
   (C) Predictable
   (D) Inconvenient
   (E) Inconsequential

   The best choice is (A). While it's true that some effects will cause inconvenience, making choice (D) a possible answer, the passage indicates that more far-reaching effects are probable as well. Another possible answer is choice (B), but according to the passage, effects will vary from place to place; *disastrous* is too strong a word and not as accurate as choice (A) *complex* (line 20). Choice (C) can be eliminated, since the passage states that the effects can't be predicted easily (lines 19-20). Choice (E) is also clearly incorrect; global warming will have significant effects (lines 24-25).

As you read, note the tone of the passage. The words that the author uses to describe events, people, or places will help give you an understanding of what and how the author wants you to feel or think. Pay careful attention to the types of words—are they emotional, calm, positive, negative, subjective, or objective?

Sample:

4. Which of the following best describes the author's tone in this passage?
   (A) Alarmist
   (B) Irate
   (C) Concerned
   (D) Accusatory
   (E) Indifferent

The best choice is (C). Although the author does mention some possible *staggering* effects, the tone is calm and concerned, not emotional as in choice (A). Nor is the tone *irate,* choice (B), or *accusatory,* choice (D); the author presents facts about fossil fuels' role in global warming but doesn't place blame. Choice (E) is also incorrect; see, for example, lines 43-45, which clearly indicate the author is not indifferent to the issue of humans' effect on global climate.

Take advantage of the line numbers. All passages have the lines numbered, which, in questions that mention specific line numbers, gives you the advantage of being able to quickly spot where the information is located. Once you spot the location, be sure to read the line(s) before and after the lines mentioned. This nearby text can be very helpful in putting the information in the proper context and answering the question.

Sample:

5. The name "greenhouse gases," first mentioned in line 62, is
   appropriate because these gases
   (A) are hot
   (B) are produced in controlled circumstances
   (C) filter the sun's harmful rays
   (D) are highly concentrated
   (E) prevent heat loss

The best choice is (E). Although *greenhouse gases* are first mentioned in line 62, the answer to the question is actually found in
lines 66-68. You can eliminate choice (B); even though it is true
that a greenhouse is a controlled climate, the gases—unlike
greenhouse plants—are not produced in a controlled climate.
Also, nothing in the passage suggests that these gases are hot,
choice (A), or that they filter out harmful rays, choice (C). While
it is true that the gases can be highly concentrated, choice (D),
high concentration has nothing to do with the term *greenhouse.*

**Use the context to figure out the meaning of words, even if you're
unfamiliar with them.** Some of the questions deal with "vocabulary in context," that is, with understanding the meaning of a word as
it is used in the passage. Even if you don't know the meaning of the
word, the passage will give you good clues. You can also read the
sentence from the passage, leaving the word space blank, and plug in
each choice to see which answer choice makes sense in the sentence.

Sample:

6. The best definition of "exacerbate" in line 41 is
   (A) worsen
   (B) change
   (C) cause
   (D) complicate
   (E) affect

The best choice is (A). As it is used in this sentence, *exacerbate* means to aggravate or irritate (make worse). The passage describes the problems as already existing; therefore, choice (C) could not be correct. From context, it is also clear that choices (B), (D), and (E) are too mild; none of them includes the concept of an existing problem (such as water quality) becoming *worse* because of variable and extreme precipitation. In this case, a common meaning is the correct answer, but remember that the common meaning of the word is not always the meaning used in the passage.

Read all the choices, since you're looking for the *best* answer given. *Best* is a relative term; that is, determining what is *best* may mean choosing from degrees of *good, better,* or *best.* Although you may have more than one good choice, you're looking for the *best* of those given. Remember, the answer doesn't have to be perfect, just the best of those presented to you. So don't get stuck on one choice before you read the rest.

Sample:

7. According to the passage, scientists are most interested in the link between global warming and extreme changes in regional climate because
   (A) such a link has never been made and cannot be easily explained
   (B) establishing the link will prove their current theories about the causes of global warming
   (C) it could help explain the effects of natural forces, such as gravitational pull, on climate
   (D) finding it will solve the problem of global warming
   (E) it could help pinpoint which human activities are involved in climate extremes

The best choice is (E). It is possible that choices (A) and (B) are peripheral reasons for their interest, but not their main reason and therefore not the *best* answer. Choice (C) is not the best answer because scientists are more interested in the effects of human activities than those of natural forces on global warming. Even though it is a step toward a solution, understanding the link wouldn't in itself *solve* the problem of global warming, thus eliminating choice (D). Notice that some of the choices here are possible, but choice (E) is the *best* because it is clearly supported in lines 54-60.

Use an elimination strategy. Often you can arrive at the right answer by eliminating other answers. Watch for key words in the answer choices to help you find the main point given in each choice. Notice that some incorrect choices are too general, too specific, irrelevant, or off topic or that they contradict information given in the passage.

Sample:

8. If true, which of the following would call into question current theories of global warming?
   (A) A dramatic increase in world precipitation
   (B) A dramatic decrease in world precipitation
   (C) An increase in the rate of global warming following the elimination of the use of fossil fuels
   (D) Below-normal temperature recordings in Canada for two years
   (E) The discovery that average global temperatures were lower 500 years ago than they are today

   The best choice is (C). Since experts believe that the use of fossil fuels is partly responsible, one would expect the elimination of that use to lead to a *decrease,* not an increase, in the rate of global warming. Both increases and decreases in precipitation are expected, and therefore choices (A) and (B) are incorrect and can be eliminated. Two years of decreased temperatures in a particular area wouldn't disprove global warming; its effects vary considerably from place to place, according to the passage; thus, choice (D) could be eliminated. Finally, you can eliminate choice (E), since it would support the theory, not call it into question.

The Questions and Key Strategies for Critical Reading Questions Based on Paired Passages

You'll be given two passages (paired passages) that have a common theme or subject. Each passage in some way relates to the other passage—sometimes supporting, sometimes opposing the views given. In some instances, the two passages are about the same subject but were written at different times—years, decades, or centuries—or in different places. You can use all of the general strategies given on page 40 for these paired passages. In addition, many of the strategies

CLIFFS QUICK REVIEW

given for single passages are also included below, but there are also some new strategies you can use for paired passages.

Specific strategies for questions based on paired passages.

- Carefully read any introductory material describing or giving information about the two passages.

- Note that the first group of questions refers to the first passage, the second group of questions refers to the second passage, and the last group of questions refers to both passages as they relate to each other.

- Consider reading the first passage, then answering the first group of questions, and then reading the second passage and answering the remaining questions.

- Be aware that the first question can (and sometimes does) ask for the primary purpose of both passages.

- Be aware of how the passages are alike and different.

- Watch out for choices that are true for one passage but not the other.

- Read the passages looking for the main point and the structure of each passage.

- Make sure that your answer is supported by the passages. Some good or true answers are not correct.

- As you read, note the tone of each passage.

- Take advantage of the line numbers.

- Use the context to figure out the meaning of words, even if you're unfamiliar with them.

- Read all the choices, since you're looking for the *best* answer given.

- Use an elimination strategy.

Paired passages and sample questions

Following is a set of "paired passages" with questions and explanations. Try your hand at marking the passages and the questions and answering the questions before you read the explanation and analysis of each.

Questions 1-14 are based on the following passages.

Both of the following passages present attitudes toward labor and leisure. Passage 1 is by the English writer Thomas Carlyle; it was published in 1843. Passage 2 is from a 1932 essay written by the English philosopher Bertrand Russell.

Passage 1

For there is a perennial nobleness, and even sacredness, in Work. Were he never so benighted, forgetful of his high calling, there is always hope in a man that actually and earnestly works; in Idleness alone is there perpetual despair.

(5)   Work, never so Mammonish*, mean, *is* in communication with Nature; the real desire to get Work done will itself lead one more and more to truth, to Nature's appointments and regulations, which are truth.

The latest Gospel in the world is, Know thy work and do
(10) it. "Know thyself:" long enough has that poor "self" of thine tormented thee; thou wilt never get to "know" it, I believe! Think it not thy business, this of knowing thyself; thou art an unknowable individual: know what thou canst work at; and work at it, like a Hercules! That will be thy better plan.

(15)   It has been written, "an endless significance lies in Work;" a man perfects himself by working. Foul jungles are cleared away, fair seedfields rise instead, and stately cities; and withal the man himself first ceases to be jungle and foul unwholesome desert thereby. Consider how, even in the meanest sorts
(20) of Labour, the whole soul of a man is composed into a kind of

  *greedily intent on getting money

          CLIFFS QUICK REVIEW

real harmony, the instant he sets himself to work! Doubt,
Desire, Sorrow, Remorse, Indignation, Despair itself, all these
like hell-dogs lie beleaguering the soul of the poor dayworker,
as of every man: but he bends himself with free valour against
(25) his task, and all these are stilled, all these shrink murmuring
far off into their caves. The man is now a man. The blessed
glow of Labour in him, is it not as purifying fire, wherein all
poison is burnt up, and of sour smoke itself there is made
bright blessed flame!

Passage 2

(30)   The fact is that moving matter about, while a certain
amount of it is necessary to our existence, is emphatically not
one of the ends of human life. If it were, we should have to
consider every navvy superior to Shakespeare. We have been
misled in this matter by two causes. One is the necessity of
(35) keeping the poor contented, which has led the rich, for thousands of years, to preach the dignity of labour, while taking
care themselves to remain undignified in this respect. The
other is the new pleasure in mechanism, which makes us
delight in the astonishing clever changes that we can produce
(40) on the earth's surface. Neither of these motives makes any
great appeal to the actual worker. If you ask him what he
thinks the best part of his life, he is not likely to say: "I enjoy
manual work because it makes me feel that I am fulfilling
man's noblest task, and because I like to think how much man
(45) can transform his planet. It is true that my body demands periods of rest, which I have to fill in as best I may, but I am never
so happy as when the morning comes and I can return to the
toil from which my contentment springs." I have never heard
working men say this sort of thing. They consider work, as it
(50) should be considered, a necessary means to a livelihood, and
it is from their leisure hours that they derive whatever happi-
ness they may enjoy.

It will be said that, while a little leisure is pleasant, men
would not know how to fill their days if they had only four
(55)   hours of work out of the twenty-four. In so far as this is true
in the modern world, it is a condemnation of our period. There
was formerly a capacity for light-heartedness and play which
has been to some extent inhibited by the cult of efficiency. The
modern man thinks that everything ought to be done for the
(60)   sake of something else, and never for its own sake. Serious-
minded persons, for example, are continually condemning the
habit of going to the cinema, and telling us that it leads the
young into crime. But all the work that goes to producing a
cinema is respectable, because it is work, and because it brings
(65)   a money profit. The notion that the desirable activities are
those that bring a profit has made everything topsy-turvy. The
butcher who provides you with meat and the baker who provides you with bread are praiseworthy, because they are making money; but when you enjoy the food they have provided,
(70)   you are merely frivolous, unless you eat only to get strength
for your work. Broadly speaking, it is felt that getting money
is good and spending money is bad. Whatever merit there may
be in the production of goods must be entirely derivative from
the advantage to be obtained by consuming them.

Questions:

1. In Passage 1, work is described as all of the following EXCEPT
   (A) a path to truth
   (B) a means of banishing disruptive emotions
   (C) significant to the world
   (D) necessary for earning a livelihood
   (E) sacred

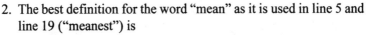

2. The best definition for the word "mean" as it is used in line 5 and line 19 ("meanest") is
   (A) malicious
   (B) intermediate
   (C) lowly
   (D) miserly
   (E) bad-tempered

3. According to information in Passage 1, with which of the following statements would the author be most likely to agree?
   (A) Work can help heal the soul.
   (B) A person who works hard will ultimately achieve success.
   (C) By balancing work and leisure a person achieves true harmony.
   (D) People can work well only when they understand the purpose of their labor.
   (E) People must labor to earn a living because of Adam and Eve's fall from grace.

4. Which of the following descriptions from Passage 1 is used to suggest the spiritual power of work?
   (A) "high calling" (lines 2-3)
   (B) "stately cities" (line 17)
   (C) "free valour" (line 24)
   (D) "purifying fire" (line 27)
   (E) "smoke" (line 28)

5. Based on his views in Passage 1, the author would be most likely to approve of
   (A) slavery
   (B) psychological counseling for dissatisfied workers
   (C) the abolition of medical insurance for employees
   (D) volunteer work projects
   (E) strong labor unions

6. According to the author of Passage 2, the dignity of labor is fre-
quently asserted in order to
   (A) keep the poor content with their lot
   (B) emphasize its spirituality
   (C) give meaning to existence
   (D) increase job productivity
   (E) belittle the rich for their laziness

7. The phrase "moving matter about" (line 30) refers to
   (A) selling
   (B) earning a living
   (C) labor
   (D) managing material
   (E) transporting goods

8. The function of lines 42-48 in Passage 2 is to
   (A) dramatize the feelings of the average worker
   (B) mimic the view that labor is noble
   (C) present the author's view in simple language
   (D) attack the view that workers can't appreciate leisure time
   (E) present a rebuttal to the author's viewpoint

9. From Passage 2, we can infer that the author believes
   (A) a shorter work day would be dangerous because workers
   wouldn't know what to do with their time
   (B) most people don't see any point to the work they do
   (C) workers' leisure time doesn't contribute tangibly to the
   economy
   (D) as a class, the rich are hypocritical
   (E) manual labor is more significant than mental labor

10. In Passage 2, the author uses people's attitudes about the cinema (lines 60-65) as an example of which of the following?
    (A) Modern leisure time is wasted in frivolous pursuits.
    (B) People are so driven by the desire for profit that they've lost the ability to enjoy themselves.
    (C) Many people irrationally value production while they condemn consumption.
    (D) Modern technology offers passive entertainment rather than light-hearted play.
    (E) Creative work such as making films is better than mindless labor.

11. Which of the following best contrasts Passage 1 and Passage 2?
    (A) Passage 1 includes only theory, whereas Passage 2 includes only facts.
    (B) In Passage 1, the author's point of view is clearly stated, whereas in Passage 2, the author expresses no point of view.
    (C) The language in Passage 1 is formal and correct, while the language in Passage 2 is filled with slang and jargon.
    (D) The view of labor in Passage 1 is more idealistic than the view in Passage 2.
    (E) Passage 1 moves from specific detail to general statement, whereas Passage 2 moves from general statement to specific detail.

12. Which of the following best describes the difference in tone between Passages 1 and 2?
    (A) Serious/playful
    (B) Optimistic/pessimistic
    (C) Sincere/insincere
    (D) Angry/ironic
    (E) Passionate/reflective

13. Which lines in Passage 2 best reflect the attitude presented in Passage 1?
    (A) Lines 32-33: ". . . we should have to consider every navvy . . . Shakespeare."
    (B) Lines 42-48: "'I enjoy manual work because . . . contentment springs.'"
    (C) Lines 53-55: "It will be said that, while a little leisure is pleasant . . . of the twenty-four."
    (D) Lines 58-60: "The modern man thinks . . . for its own sake."
    (E) Lines 72-74: "Whatever merit there may be . . . consuming them."

14. Based on the passages, with which of the following statements would both authors be most likely to agree?
    (A) An activity shouldn't be judged solely on its potential for making a profit.
    (B) A machine should never replace a human being in the workplace because a machine has no soul.
    (C) Humans are basically evil.
    (D) Humans are basically good.
    (E) When people are idle, they brood on the misery in their lives.

An analysis of the paired-passage questions. The first questions usually refer to the first passage. **Notice that the first five questions in this set refer to Passage 1.** In the following analysis, the task required by each of the questions is identified first.

Describing a word, phrase, or concept.

1. The best choice is (D). First underline or circle the words *work is described as.* The author writes of the dignity of work and its importance to a person's state of mind, but he doesn't address the

necessity of earning a living. You might be tempted to choose (C) because the emphasis is on the benefit of work to the individual's state of mind rather than its benefit to the world; however, notice lines 16-17. Choices (A), (B), and (E) are all mentioned in the passage (lines 6-7, lines 21-26, and line 1).

Defining a word or words from context.

2. The best choice is (C). First underline or circle the words *definition, mean,* and *meanest.* While the word *mean* has several definitions—including those listed here—in the context of the passage, *lowly* makes the most sense. The author is extolling the virtues of all labor, regardless of how important or dignified it may be. The other definitions don't fit as well. In addition, choices (A), (D), and (E) are more appropriately applied to humans. Choice (B) doesn't make sense; what would *intermediate work* mean?

Deciding with which statement the author would most likely agree.

3. The best choice is (A); see lines 21-26. First underline or circle *author be most likely to agree.* Choices (B) and (D) are irrelevant; the author doesn't consider work in these terms, and although he might agree with choice (B), the passage doesn't indicate this. Instead, the author stresses work's spiritual values. Choice (C) is incorrect; according to the passage, harmony is achieved through work alone, and *Idleness* leads to despair. Choice (E) is not addressed in the passage; the author sees work as a blessing, not a curse.

Identifying what a description suggests.

4. The best choice is (D). First underline or circle *descriptions . . . suggest the spiritual power of work.* (The word *purifying* is a good clue.) Choice (B) suggests the practical results of work but

not its spiritual significance. Choice (C) describes the state of workers as they address their tasks, and choice (A) describes humans' purpose on earth, not the significance of work. Choice (E) is incorrect; *sour smoke* refers to the state of the human soul before the *purifying fire* of work.

Recognizing which statement an author would be likely to approve of.

5. The best choice is (D). First underline or circle *author . . . approve.* The author values work in terms of its effects on the worker's soul rather than its effects on his or her pocketbook. He wouldn't be likely to approve of slavery, choice (A); notice that the dayworker he describes in lines 23-24 *bends himself with free valour.* It is also unlikely he would approve of choice (B); see lines 10-13. Nothing in the passage suggests that he would oppose medical benefits for workers, choice (C), or approve of labor unions, choice (E).

Notice that these next five questions refer to Passage 2.

Determining why certain items are asserted.

6. The best choice is (A) (lines 34-37). First underline or circle *dignity of labor is frequently asserted in order to.* Choices (B) and (C) contradict the author's point that this assertion is made for ulterior motives and that people who actually work for a living do so to earn their livelihood, not to gain spiritually or give meaning to their lives. Choice (D) may seem a possible answer, but it is irrelevant to this passage. Choice (E) may also be the reason some people assert the dignity of labor—but it isn't the reason given in the passage; in fact, the author states that it is the rich themselves who make the assertion for their own purposes.

Identifying what a phrase refers to.

7. The best choice is (C). First underline or circle *moving matter about*. Although moving matter about may be the way that people earn a living, choice (B), the phrase describes the labor itself, not the *reason* for it. Choices (A), (D), and (E) are too narrow in scope. The phrase is used figuratively to encompass labor in general.

Identifying the function of certain lines.

8. The best choice is (B). You should first underline or circle *function* (and possibly *lines 42-48*). The author's intention is to mimic a traditional view, which—in his opinion—is opposite to the actual view of workers. Therefore, choices (A) and (C) are both incorrect. Choices (D) and (E) are both irrelevant; these lines don't attack or rebut any viewpoint.

Making an inference concerning a belief of the author.

9. The best choice is (D). See lines 34-37. Underline or circle *infer . . . author believes.* Choice (B) may be tempting, but the author makes it clear that people do see a point to their work: earning a living. Choices (C) and (E) are not correct inferences. According to the author, consumption (which includes leisure-time activities) is necessary to production. Lines 32-33 contradict choice (E). Choice (A) expresses a common objection to the argument for a shorter work day, not the author's own opinion.

Deciding what an author's example refers to.

10. The best choice is (C). First underline or circle *author, uses,* and *example.* The author says that people condemn the habit of going to the cinema (consumption) but see the work going into making movies as respectable (production). Choices (A), (D), and (E) are

irrelevant; the quality of neither work nor leisure activities is judged. While choice (B) represents an idea suggested in the passage, the double attitude toward the cinema is better stated in choice (C).

Notice that the next four questions refer to both passages.

Identifying a statement that contrasts the passages.

11. The best choice is (D). Underline or circle *contrasts.* In Passage 1, labor is shown more idealistically—for example, in *a man perfects himself by working,* and *the whole soul of a man is composed into a kind of real harmony.* Compare these descriptions to lines 48-52 in Passage 2. Choice (A) is incorrect; Passage 2 doesn't present facts, but rather opinions. Passage 2 isn't filled with slang and jargon, choice (C), and although the style is less emphatic than the author's style in Passage 1, a point of view is clear, choice (B). Choice (E) is simply incorrect; it describes the movement of neither passage.

Choosing a correct description of a difference in tone.

12. The best choice is (E). First underline or circle *difference in tone.* While the author of Passage 2 uses humor and irony and the author of Passage 1 doesn't, Passage 2 isn't playful, choice (A). The tone of Passage 1 is passionate, but it isn't angry, choice (D). Choice (B) is incorrect; neither passage is clearly optimistic or pessimistic. The sincerity or insincerity of the passages, choice (C), depends on the eye of the beholder, not on anything intrinsic to the passages.

Identifying a line or lines in a passage that best reflect a particular attitude.

13. The best choice is (B). First underline or circle *reflect the attitude*. The author of Passage 2 is mimicking (and therefore reflecting) the point of view in Passage 1. Passage 1 doesn't compare modern humans to their predecessors, choice (D); nor does it consider the value of consumption, choice (E). Also, choice (C) doesn't accurately describe his attitude toward *Idleness*. Choice (A) may seem the best answer, but while the author of Passage 1 extols the virtues of all labor, no matter how menial, he doesn't indicate that moving goods is *superior* to creating literature.

Determining on what point the authors would be likely to agree.

14. The best choice is (A). First underline or circle *authors be most likely to agree*. Notice lines 5-8 and 19-21 in Passage 1 and lines 56-60 and 65-66 in Passage 2. The author of Passage 2 wouldn't agree with choice (B); he might object to a machine's robbing people of their livelihood, but he wouldn't reject a machine because it had no soul. Choices (C) and (D) are incorrect; there is insufficient information in the passages to determine the authors' beliefs about humans' good or evil nature. The author of Passage 1 would agree with choice (E), but the author of Passage 2 would not (lines 48-52).

Three Final Strategies for Any Passage

If you're having real trouble with a passage or simply running out of time, try one of these three strategies.

Skip a difficult passage. You could skip a difficult passage entirely, along with the questions based on it, and come back to them later.

Remember that you can return to those questions only while you're working in that section. Also, if you use this strategy, take care to mark your answers in the correct spaces on the answer sheet when you skip a group of questions.

Skim the passage. If you're running out of time, you might want to skim the passage and then answer the questions—referring back to the passage when necessary.

Potshot questions and spots in the passage. For this "last resort method," simply read the questions that refer to specific lines in the passage and read only those specific lines in the passage (potshot them) to try to answer the question. This final strategy may help you at least eliminate some answer choices and take some educated guesses.

THE BASICS, THE QUESTIONS, AND THE KEY
STRATEGIES FOR MATHEMATICAL REASONING

The Skills You'll Use

The Mathematical Reasoning sections test your ability to solve mathematical problems involving

- arithmetic
- algebra
- geometry
- word problems

by using

- problem-solving insight
- logic
- reasoning
- application of basic math skills

You also need to quickly interpret information and make mathematical comparisons.

The Types of Questions

Mathematical Reasoning is composed of three basic types of questions:

- regular multiple-choice questions
- quantitative comparison questions
- grid-in questions

Yor Mathematical Reasoning Score

Three Mathematical Reasoning sections count toward your score: a 30-minute section that contains 25 multiple-choice questions; another 30-minute section that contains 15 quantitative comparison questions and 10 grid-in questions (25 questions total); and finally a 15-minute section that contains 10 multiple-choice questions.

Although the order of the sections and the number of questions may change, the three sections currently total 60 math questions. A scaled score from 200 to 800 is generated by these three sections (60 questions). About 50% right should generate an average score (approximately 500).

Mathematical Reasoning

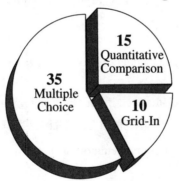

(approximately 60 questions
that count toward your score)

The Levels of Difficulty

The math sections are slightly graduated in difficulty. That is, the easiest questions are generally at the beginning, and the more difficult ones at the end. If a section has two types of questions, then each type usually starts with easier problems. For example, a section starts with easy quantitative comparison questions and progresses to more difficult ones before the beginning of the grid-in questions. Then the grid-in questions start with easier questions and move toward more difficult ones at the end.

You'll receive reference information preceding each Mathematical Reasoning section. You should be familiar with this information.

Using Your Calculator

The SAT I allows the use of calculators, and the College Board (the people who sponsor the exam) recommends that each test taker bring a calculator to the test. Even though no question will require the use of a calculator—that is, each question can be answered without one—in some instances, using a calculator will save you valuable time.

You should

- Bring your own calculator, since you can't borrow one during the exam.

- Bring a calculator even if you don't think you'll use it.

- Make sure that you're familiar with the use of your calculator.

- Make sure that your calculator has new, fresh batteries and is in good working order.

- Practice using your calculator on some of the problems to see when and where it will be helpful.

- Check for a shortcut in any problem that seems to involve much computation. But use your calculator if it will be time effective. If there appears to be too much computation or the problem seems impossible to solve without using the calculator, you're probably doing something wrong.

- Before doing an operation, check the number that you keyed in on the display to make sure that you keyed in the right number. You may wish to check each number as you key it in.

- Before using your calculator, set up the problem and/or steps on your paper. Write the numbers on paper as you perform each step on your calculator. (It is generally safer not to use the memory function on your calculator.)

- Be sure to carefully clear the calculator before beginning new calculations.

Be careful that you

- Don't rush out and buy a sophisticated calculator for the test.

- Don't bring a calculator that you're unfamiliar with.

- Don't bring a pocket organizer, hand-held mini-computer, laptop computer, or calculator with a typewriter-type keypad or paper tape.

- Don't bring a calculator that requires an outlet or any other external power source.

- Don't bring a calculator that makes noise.

- Don't try to share a calculator.

- Don't try to use a calculator on every problem.

- Don't become dependent on your calculator.

Take advantage of being allowed to use a calculator on the test. Learn to use your calculator efficiently by practicing. As you approach a problem, first focus on how to solve that problem, and then decide if the calculator will be helpful. Remember, a calculator can save you time on some problems, but also remember that each problem can be solved without one. Also remember that a calculator will not solve a problem for you by itself. You must understand the problem first.

Basic Skills and Concepts You Should Be Familiar With

Arithmetic

- Operations with fractions

- Applying addition, subtraction, multiplication, and division to problem solving

- Arithmetic mean (average), mode, and median

- Ratio and proportion

- Number properties: positive and negative integers, odd and even numbers, prime numbers, factors and multiples, divisibility

- Word problems: solving for percents, averages, rate, time, distance, interest, price per item

- Number lines: order, consecutive numbers, fractions, betweenness

Algebra

- Operations with signed numbers

- Substitution for variables

- Working with algebraic expressions

- Word problems

- Solving equations

- Solving inequalities

- Basic factoring

- Working with positive exponents

- Working with positive roots

- Elementary quadratic equations

Geometry

- Vertical angles

- Angles in figures
- Perpendicular and parallel lines
- Perimeter, area, angle measure of polygons
- Circumference, area, radius, diameter
- Triangles: right, isosceles, equilateral, angle measure, similarity
- Special triangles: $30°-60°-90°, 45°-45°-90°$
- Pythagorean theorem
- Volume and surface area of solids
- Coordinate geometry: coordinates, slope

Other Topics

- Interpreting graphs, charts, and tables
- Sequence problems
- Probability
- Special symbols, or false operations
- Reasoning problems

On the Mathematical Reasoning sections, you will have

- No time-consuming and tedious computations
- No fractional exponents
- No use of the quadratic formula
- No complicated roots and radicals
- No geometric proofs

Reference Information

The information on the following page is given to you for reference before each math section of the exam.

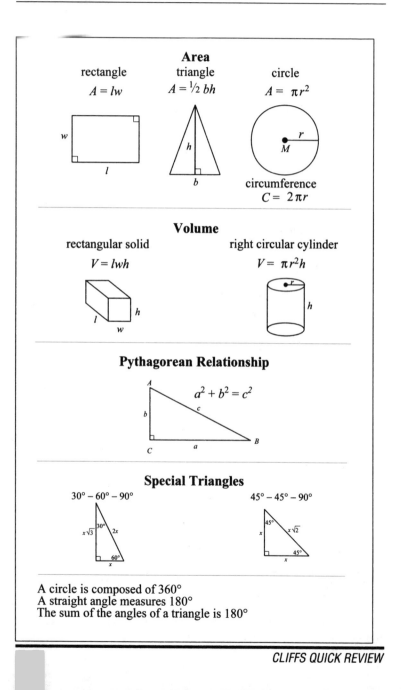

Area

rectangle

$A = lw$

triangle

$A = \frac{1}{2} bh$

circle

$A = \pi r^2$

circumference

$C = 2\pi r$

Volume

rectangular solid

$V = lwh$

right circular cylinder

$V = \pi r^2 h$

Pythagorean Relationship

$a^2 + b^2 = c^2$

Special Triangles

$30° - 60° - 90°$

$45° - 45° - 90°$

A circle is composed of 360°
A straight angle measures 180°
The sum of the angles of a triangle is 180°

The Basics of Multiple-Choice Math Questions

The number of questions. You should have a total of 35 multiple-choice math questions that count toward your score—25 in one 30-minute section and 10 in a 15-minute section.

The directions. Solve each problem in this section by using the information given and your own mathematical calculations, insights, and problem-solving skills. Then select the one correct answer of the five choices given and mark the corresponding circle on your answer sheet. Use the available space on the page for your scratch work.

Notes

(1) All numbers used are real numbers.
(2) Calculators may be used.
(3) Some problems may be accompanied by figures or diagrams. These figures are drawn as accurately as possible except when it is stated in a specific problem that a figure is not drawn to scale. The figures and diagrams are meant to provide information useful in solving the problem or problems. Unless otherwise stated, all figures and diagrams lie in a plane.

The Questions and Key Strategies for Multiple-Choice Math

- Underline or circle what you're looking for.
- Simplify the problem.
- Work forward.

- Work backward, from the answers.
- Plug in simple numbers.
- Pull out information.
- Mark in, or fill in, the diagram.
- If no diagram is given, draw one.
- Note that some diagrams are not drawn to scale.
- Use 10 or 100.
- Approximate.
- Glance at the choices on procedure problems.
- Be reasonable.

Underline or circle what you're looking for. Take advantage of being allowed to mark in the test booklet by always underlining or circling what you're looking for so you're sure that you're answering the right question.

Sample:

1. If $3y + 21 = 30$, then $y + 7 =$
   (A) 3   (B) 5   (C) 9   (D) 10   (E) 16

   You should first underline or circle " $y + 7$ " because that's what you're solving for. Focusing on $y + 7$ may give you the insight to simply divide the complete equation by 3, giving you $y + 7 = 10$. This is the fastest method, but if you don't spot the shortcut, you could solve for y and then add 7. If you solve for y, you would first subtract 21 from each side.

$$3y + 21 = 30$$
$$ -21 \;\; -21$$
$$\overline{3y \;\;\; = \;\;\; 9}$$

Dividing each side by 3 gives $y = 3$.

At this point you could easily select the most common wrong answer, choice (A). But since you circled $y + 7$, you're reminded to add 7 to your answer, giving you the correct answer of 10, choice (D). *Make sure that you're answering the right question.*

Simplify the problem. Sometimes combining terms, performing simple operations, or simplifying the problem in some other way will give you insight and make the problem easier to solve.

Sample:

2. $(2 + 7)^3 =$
    (A) $2 \times 3 + 7 \times 3$
    (B) $2^3 + 7^3$
    (C) $2 \times 2 \times 2 + 7 \times 7 \times 7$
    (D) $2^3 \times 7^3$
    (E) 9^3

Simplifying this problem first means adding the two numbers inside the parentheses, which gives you $(9)^3$, or 9^3, which is choice (E). *Notice that simplifying can make a problem easier to solve and can lead directly to a correct answer.*

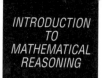

INTRODUCTION
TO
MATHEMATICAL
REASONING

Work forward. If you immediately recognize the method or proper formula to solve the problem, then do the work. Work forward.

Sample:

3. Which of the following numbers is between $\frac{1}{3}$ and $\frac{1}{4}$?

(A) .45   (B) .35   (C) .29   (D) .22   (E) .20

You should first underline or circle "between $\frac{1}{3}$ and $\frac{1}{4}$." If you know that $\frac{1}{3}$ is .333 . . . and $\frac{1}{4}$ is .25, you have insight into the problem and should simply work it forward. Since .29 is the only number between .333 . . . and .25, the correct answer is (C). By the way, a quick peek at the answer choices would tip you off that you should work in decimals.

Work backward, from the answers. If you don't immediately recognize a method or formula, or if using the method or formula would take a great deal of time, try working backward—from the answers. Since the answers are usually given in ascending or descending order, always start by plugging in answer (C) first. Then you'll know whether to go up or down with your next try. (Sometimes you might want to plug in one of the simple answers first.)

Sample:

4. If $\frac{x}{2} + \frac{3}{4} = 1\frac{1}{4}$, what is the value of x?

(A) −2   (B) −1   (C) 0   (D) 1   (E) 2

You should first underline or circle "value of x." If you've forgotten how to solve this kind of equation, work backward by plugging in answers. Start with choice (C); plug in 0.

$$\frac{0}{2} + \frac{3}{4} \neq 1\frac{1}{4}$$

CLIFFS QUICK REVIEW

Since this answer is too small, try choice (D), a larger number. Plugging in 1 gives.

$$\frac{1}{2} + \frac{3}{4} \stackrel{?}{=} 1\frac{1}{4}$$

$$\frac{2}{4} + \frac{3}{4} \stackrel{?}{=} 1\frac{1}{4}$$

$$\frac{5}{4} = 1\frac{1}{4}$$

This answer is true, so (D) is the correct answer. *Working from the answers is a valuable technique.*

Plug in simple numbers. Substituting numbers for variables can often help in understanding a problem. Remember to plug in *simple, small* numbers, since you have to do the work.

Sample:

5. If *r* represents an even integer, then an odd integer is represented by which of the following?
   (A) $3r$
   (B) $2r + 1$
   (C) $3r + 2$
   (D) $4r - 2$
   (E) $5r - 4$

Since the question says that "*r* represents an even integer," substitute 2 for *r*. You should underline or circle "an odd integer" because that's what you're looking for. So as you plug 2 into each choice, you can stop when you get an odd integer.

$$\text{(A) } 3r = 3(2) = 6$$

$$\text{(B) } 2r + 1 = 2(2) + 1 = 4 + 1 = 5$$

Since 5 is an odd integer, the correct answer is (B).

Pull out information. Pulling information out of the word problem structure can often give you a better look at what you're working with; therefore, you gain additional insight into the problem.

Sample:

6. If the ratio of boys to girls in a drama class is 2 to 1, which of the following is a possible number of students in the class?
   (A) 10   (B) 16   (C) 19   (D) 25   (E) 30

You should first underline or circle "possible number of students." Now, pulling out information gives you the following.

$$b : g = 2 : 1$$

Since the ratio of boys to girls is 2 : 1, then the possible total number of students in the class must be a multiple of 2 + 1 (boys plus girls), or 3. The multiples of 3 are 3, 6, 9, 12, 15 . . . Only choice (E) 30 is a multiple of 3.

Mark in, or fill in, the diagram. Marking in diagrams as you read the questions can save you valuable time. Marking can also give you insight into how to solve a problem because you'll have the complete picture clearly in front of you.

Sample:

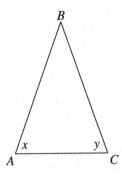

7. In the isosceles triangle above, $AB = BC$, and $\angle x$ is 70°. What is the value of $\angle y$?

 (A) 50   (B) 60   (C) 70   (D) 100   (E) 130

First underline or circle what you're looking for, " $\angle y$. " Next, in the isosceles triangle, immediately mark in that AB and BC are equal. Then mark in $\angle x$ as 70°. Since $AB = BC$, then $\angle x = \angle y$ (angles opposite equal sides are equal). After you mark in the information, your diagram should look like this.

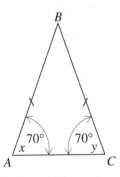

The correct choice is (C) 70, since $\angle x = \angle y$.

If no diagram is given, draw one. Sketching diagrams or simple pictures can also be helpful in problem solving because the diagram may tip you off to either a simple solution or a method for solving the problem.

Sample:

8. If the area of one face of a cube is 16 square inches, what is the volume of the cube in cubic inches?

    (A) 8   (B) 12   (C) 24   (D) 64   (E) 96

First underline or circle the word "volume." Now draw a cube.

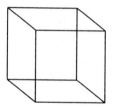

Next label one face of the cube. This should help you determine that each edge of the cube is 4, since the face of a cube is a square and all edges are equal.

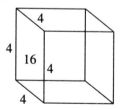

The formula for the volume of a cube is length times width times height, or

$$v = lwh$$

So the volume is

$$4 \times 4 \times 4 = 64$$

which is choice (D).

Note that some diagrams are not drawn to scale. Figures and diagrams are drawn as accurately as possible, unless a diagram is labeled "not drawn to scale." That label is a tip-off that the diagram could be drawn differently or is out of proportion. So you should mark the diagram and quickly redraw it *differently*. Redrawing will give you insight into what information you really have about the diagram.

Sample:

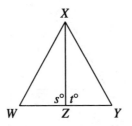

Note: Figure not drawn to scale.

9. In $\triangle WXY$ above, $WX = XY$. Which of the following must be true?
   (A) $WZ = ZY$
   (B) $s = t$
   (C) perimeter of $\triangle WXZ$ = perimeter of $\triangle ZXY$
   (D) area of $\triangle WXZ$ = area of $\triangle ZXY$
   (E) $\angle XWZ = \angle XYZ$

Before doing anything else, underline or circle "must be true." Now mark the diagram as follows.

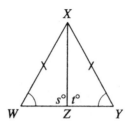

Next, since the figure is *not* drawn to scale, quickly redraw it another way that still conforms to the given information.

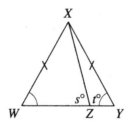

Notice that by looking at the way the figure is initially drawn, you might think that $WZ = ZY$ because they appear to be equal. But once you redraw the figure, you can see that WZ and ZY don't have to be equal, eliminating choice (A).

The same can be noticed of s and t. They don't have to be equal, eliminating choice (B).

A quick look at your redrawn figure will help you eliminate choice (C) as well, since it's evident that triangles WXZ and ZXY don't necessarily have equal perimeters.

You can also eliminate choice (D) because even though the heights of triangles *WXZ* and *ZXY* are equal, their bases could be different, so the areas could be different. This fact is also evident from your redrawing of the diagram.

Choice (E) is the correct answer because in any triangle, equal angles are across from equal sides. Your markings in the figure remind you that this is true.

Use 10 or 100. Some problems may deal with percent or percent change. If you don't see a simple method for working the problem, try using values of 10 or 100 and see what you get.

Sample:

10. If 40% of the students in a class have blue eyes and 20% of those with blue eyes have brown hair, then what percent of the original total number have brown hair and blue eyes?
    (A) 4%   (B) 8%   (C) 16%   (D) 20%   (E) 32%

    First underline or circle "percent of the original total number . . . brown hair . . . blue eyes." In this problem, if you don't spot a simple method, try starting with 100 students in the class. Since 40% of them have blue eyes, then 40 students have blue eyes. Now, the problem says that 20% of those students with blue eyes have brown hair. So take 20% of 40, which gives you

$$.20 \times 40 = 8$$

    Since the question asks what percent of the original total number have blue eyes and brown hair, and since you started with 100 students, the answer is choice (B), 8 out of 100, or 8%.

Approximate. If it appears that extensive calculations are going to be necessary to solve a problem, check to see how far apart the choices are and then approximate. The reason for checking the answers first is to give you a guide to see how freely you can approximate.

Sample:

11. If 2,100 people work in a factory, and 21% of them work only the night shift, approximately how many people work the other shifts?
    (A) 400   (B) 800   (C) 1,100   (D) 1,600   (E) 2,000

    First underline or circle "approximately how many people . . . other shifts." Remember, you're looking for "other shifts." Notice that the answers are spread out. Approximate 21% as 20% and 2,100 as 2,000. Now, 20% of 2,000 is 400. But be careful; this is the number of those who work only the night shift. You want those who work the other shifts. So you must subtract 400 from 2,000, leaving 1,600, choice (D).

    Another method is to, after approximating, subtract 20% from 100%, which gives you 80%, which is the percent of other workers. Now multiply 80% times 2,000 and you get 1,600.

Glance at the choices on procedure problems. Some problems may not ask you to solve for a numerical answer or even an answer including variables. Rather, you may be asked to set up the equation or expression without doing any solving. A quick glance at the answer choices will help you know what is expected. If any information is given in a box, read the question first—that is, before reading the information in the box.

Sample:

> The number w is twice the number z.
> The difference between w and z is 4.

12. Which of the pairs of equations that follow could be used to solve for w and z?
    (A) $w = 2z; w - z = 4$
    (B) $2w = z; w - z = 4$
    (C) $w = z + 2; w - z = 4$
    (D) $w = 2z; w + z = 4$
    (E) $w = z - 2; w + z = 4$

First read the question and underline or circle "equations . . . could be used to solve." Next read the information in the box. Now you can quickly set up two equations from the information given in the box and then compare your equations to the choices.

The number w is twice the number z.
$$w = 2z$$

Notice that this equation eliminates choices (B), (C), and (E).

The difference between w and z is 4.
$$w - z = 4$$

The correct answer is choice (A), $w = 2z$ and $w - z = 4$.

Be reasonable. Sometimes a reasonable approach will save you time or help you eliminate wrong answers that result from common mistakes. If no mathematical method comes to mind, try a reasonable approach. Also, after solving, always check to see that the answer is actually reasonable.

Sample:

13. Will can complete a job in 30 minutes. Eli can complete the same job in 60 minutes. If they work together, approximately how many minutes will it take them to complete the job?
   (A) 90   (B) 60   (C) 45   (D) 30   (E) 20

First underline or circle "work together, approximately how many minutes." In a reasonable approach, you'd reason that since Will can complete the job alone in 30 minutes, then if he receives any help, the job should take less than 30 minutes. He's receiving a fair amount of help, so the answer must be well below 30 minutes. The only answer below 30 is choice (E) 20.

The Basics of Quantitative Comparison Questions

The number of questions. You should have 15 quantitative comparison questions. They typically will be the first 15 questions in a 30-minute section that includes about 10 grid-in questions, as well.

The directions. In this section, you will be given two quantities, one in column A and one in column B. You are to determine a relationship between the two quantities and mark—

(A) if the quantity in column A is greater than the quantity in column B

(B) if the quantity in column B is greater than the quantity in column A

(C) if the quantities are equal

(D) if the comparison cannot be determined from the information that is given

AN (E) RESPONSE WILL NOT BE SCORED.

Notes

(1) Sometimes, information concerning one or both of the quantities to be compared is given. This information is not boxed and is centered above the two columns.

(2) All numbers used are real numbers. Letters such as a, b, m, and x represent real numbers.

(3) In a given question, if the same symbol is used in column A and column B, that symbol stands for the same value in each column.

The Questions and Key Strategies for Quantitative Comparison

- Look for a quick method.
- Check each column before working.
- Watch the sign (+, −) in each column.
- Note if the columns increase or decrease.
- Substitute in simple numbers: 0, 1, −1, 2, 10 (maybe $\frac{1}{2}$)
- Simplify columns if possible.
- Compare part by part.
- Solve a problem directly, if possible.
- Determine what information is needed.
- Read the center information carefully.
- Mark in, or fill in, the diagram.
- If no diagram is given, draw one.
- Note that some diagrams are not drawn to scale.
- Use familiar numbers.

Look for a quick method. The quantitative comparison section emphasizes shortcuts, insight, and quick techniques. Long and/or involved mathematical computation is unnecessary and is contrary to the purpose of this section. *If the problem takes too long, you're probably doing it wrong.*

Sample:

Column A	Column B

1.

$$\frac{1}{2} \times \frac{1}{5} \times \frac{3}{8} \qquad\qquad \frac{1}{5} \times \frac{1}{2} \times \frac{5}{13}$$

Before doing all of the work, look for a quick method. In this case, cancel each side as follows.

$$\cancel{\frac{1}{2}} \times \cancel{\frac{1}{5}} \times \frac{3}{8} \qquad\qquad \cancel{\frac{1}{5}} \times \cancel{\frac{1}{2}} \times \frac{5}{13}$$

which leaves

$$\frac{3}{8} \qquad\qquad\qquad\qquad \frac{5}{13}$$

The quickest way to compare two fractions is to cross-multiply upwards. Notice that whichever number has the greater number above it after cross-multiplying is the greater fraction.

$$\overset{39}{\frac{3}{8}} \diagup \overset{40}{\frac{5}{13}}$$

Since 40 is greater than 39, $\frac{5}{13}$ is greater than $\frac{3}{8}$. The correct answer is (B), column B is greater.

Check each column before working. Always keep the columns in perspective before starting any calculations. Take a good look at the value in each column before starting to work on one column.

Sample:

Column A	Column B
2.	20% of 520	50% of 500

In looking at each column, you should be able to quickly notice that 20% of 520 is much less than 50% of 500. If you check each column, you can make the comparison without doing any actual math computations. The correct answer is (B), column B is greater.

Another sample:

Column A	Column B
3.	$\frac{1}{2} \times \frac{1}{4} \times \frac{1}{3}$	$.5 \times .25 \times .3$

By quickly checking each column, you should notice that $\frac{1}{2}$ in column A is the same as .5 in column B. You should also notice that $\frac{1}{4}$ in column A is the same as .25 in column B.

$$\cancel{\frac{1}{2}} \times \cancel{\frac{1}{4}} \times \frac{1}{3} \qquad\qquad \cancel{.5} \times \cancel{.25} \times .3$$

So you're actually comparing $\frac{1}{3}$ and .3. Since $\frac{1}{3}$ is .333 . . ., column A is greater, so the answer is (A).

Watch the sign (+, –) in each column. As you keep each column in perspective, notice if the signs (+, –) *produced by the computations* in each column are different. If they are, then you don't need to work out the problem.

Sample:

Column A	Column B
$(-3)^7$	$(-2)^4$

4.

Notice that the value in column A will always be negative, since a negative number to an odd power is always negative. The value in column B will always be positive, since a negative number to an even power is always positive. Since all positive numbers are greater than all negative numbers, the answer is (B), column B is greater. *Note the difference* between $(-2)^4$ and -2^4.

$$(-2)^4 \text{ means } (-2) \times (-2) \times (-2) \times (-2) = 16$$
$$-2^4 \text{ means } -(2 \times 2 \times 2 \times 2) = -16$$

Another sample:

Column A   **Column B**

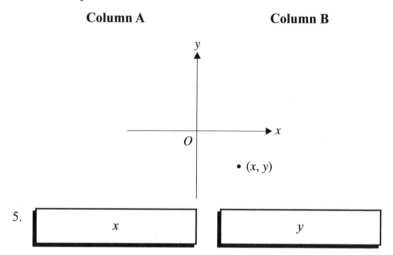

5.

| x | y |

Since the coordinates (x, y) are in quadrant IV, the x value is positive and the y value is negative. Since column A is positive and column B is negative, the correct answer is (A), column A is greater.

Note if the columns increase or decrease. Again, as you keep the columns in perspective, check to see if the values in each column increase or decrease from the starting point.

Sample:

Column A   **Column B**

6.

| $(1.1)^9$ | $(0.9)^{11}$ |

Notice that column A starts out greater than column B, since 1.1 is greater than 0.9. Column A, $(1.1)^9$, will continue to get larger (a number greater than 1 multiplied by itself gets larger), but column B, $(0.9)^{11}$, will continue to get smaller (a fraction multiplied by another fraction gets smaller). Since column A started out larger than column B and continues to get larger and column B started out smaller than column A and continues to get smaller, the answer is (A), column A is greater.

Substitute in simple numbers: 0, 1, –1, 2, 10 (maybe $\frac{1}{2}$). If a problem involves variables (without an equation), substitute in the numbers 0, 1, and –1. Then try $\frac{1}{2}$, 2, or 10 if necessary. Using these numbers will often tip you off to the answer quickly.

Sample:

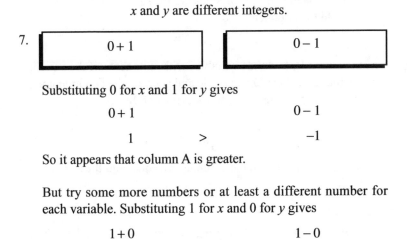

Column A **Column B**

x and y are different integers.

7.

$0 + 1$ $0 - 1$

Substituting 0 for x and 1 for y gives

$0 + 1$ $0 - 1$

1 $>$ -1

So it appears that column A is greater.

But try some more numbers or at least a different number for each variable. Substituting 1 for x and 0 for y gives

$1 + 0$ $1 - 0$

1 $=$ 1

Now it appears that the columns are equal.

*Anytime you get more than one comparison (different relation-
ships) depending on the values you choose, the correct answer
is (D), the relationship cannot be determined.*

Simplify columns if possible. Often, simplifying one or both
columns can make an answer evident.

Sample:

Column A	Column B

$$x \neq 0$$

8.

$(x^2)(x^3)$	$\dfrac{x^{11}}{x^6}$

Simplify each column. In column A, to multiply two variables
with exponents, if the variables are the same, keep the variable
and add the exponents. So

$$(x^2)(x^3) = x^5$$

In column B, to divide variables with exponents, if the variables
are the same, keep the variable and subtract the denominator's
exponent from the numerator's exponent. So

$$\frac{x^{11}}{x^6} = x^5$$

It is now evident that the columns are equal and the answer
is (C).

Compare part by part. Using partial comparisons can be valuable
in giving you insight into finding a comparison. If you can't simply
make a complete comparison, compare each column part by part.

Sample:

Column A	**Column B**
$\frac{1}{14} - \frac{1}{68}$	$\frac{1}{12} - \frac{1}{70}$

9.

You could find a common denominator and then do the calculations, but that would be time consuming. Instead, try comparing the first fraction in each column (partial comparison). Notice that $\frac{1}{14}$ is smaller than $\frac{1}{12}$. Now compare the second fractions and notice that $\frac{1}{68}$ is greater than $\frac{1}{70}$. Using some common sense and insight, you'll see that if you start with a smaller number and subtract a larger number, the result must be smaller than if you start with a larger number and subtract a smaller number. This comparison is shown below.

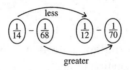

The correct answer is (B), column B is greater.

Solve a problem directly, if possible. Sometimes a second look at a problem will give you insight so that you can solve it directly (getting the value of one column easily), without doing all of the work.

Sample:

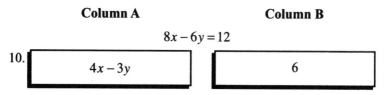

Column A	Column B
$8x - 6y = 12$	
10. $4x - 3y$	6

A careful look at column A and a second look at the original equation should tip you off that you can solve this directly. Notice that column A, $4x - 3y$, is half of $8x - 6y$. Since $8x - 6y = 12$, then $4x - 3y = 6$. So the two columns are equal, answer (C).

Determine what information is needed. Check to see if you actually have enough information to make a comparison. Be aware of the information you are given and what you need.

Sample:

Column A	Column B
Rajiv and Sal each purchase holiday gifts for his family. Rajiv spends $50, and Sal spends $40.	
11. Number of gifts purchased by Rajiv	Number of gifts purchased by Sal

First underline or circle the word "number" in each column. Since you don't know the cost of the individual gifts, you have no way to know how many gifts each purchased. The correct answer is (D), no comparison can be determined.

The common mistake would be to think that since Rajiv spends more money, he must have purchased more gifts. But that would not necessarily be the case because Rajiv may have bought more expensive (but fewer) gifts, and Sal may have bought less expensive (but more) gifts.

Read the center information carefully. Information given in the center, above the actual question, applies to the question and the columns to be compared. Read and/or work through the center information carefully.

Sample:

Column A	**Column B**

m and n are integers.

$$0 < m < n < 5$$

12.

mn	$m+n$

After taking a careful look at the center information, you realize that you are limited in the numbers you can use for m and n. So try some possibilities within these limitations.

Substituting 1 for m and 2 for n gives

$1(2)$	$1+2$
2	3

$$2 < 3$$

So when you use these numbers, column B is greater.

Now try some other possible numbers. Substituting 3 for *m* and 4 for *n*, you get

3(4)		3 + 4
12	>	7

So when you use these numbers, column A is greater

So the correct answer is (D), no comparison can be determined.

Remember, anytime you get more than one comparison (different relationships) depending on the values you choose, the correct answer is (D), the relationship cannot be determined.

Mark in, or fill in, the diagram. Marking diagrams can be very helpful in giving you insight into a problem.

Sample:

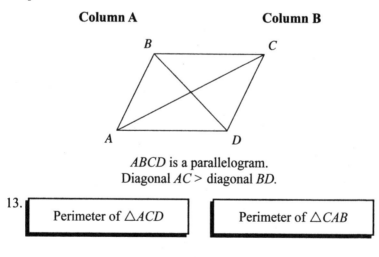

Column A   **Column B**

ABCD is a parallelogram.
Diagonal *AC* > diagonal *BD*.

13.

Perimeter of △*ACD*	Perimeter of △*CAB*

From the information given, quickly mark the diagram as follows.

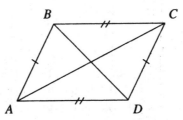

Notice that since this is a parallelogram, opposite sides are equal. Mark these sides equal. And since each triangle uses diagonal *AC,* the perimeters of the two triangles are also equal. The correct answer is (C).

If no diagram is given, draw one. Drawing diagrams can be helpful in giving you insight into a problem or tipping you off to a simple solution. If you're given a description or a geometry problem without a diagram or figure, you should make a sketch.

Sample:

Column A	Column B
14. Length of one side of a square with area of 49	Length of rectangle with area of 40 and width of 5

Simply draw and label each figure as follows.

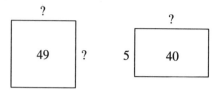

From the drawings, you can quickly find that the length of one side of the square is 7 and the length of the rectangle is 8. So the correct answer is (B), column B is greater.

Note that some diagrams are not drawn to scale. When a note is given that a figure is not drawn to scale, you're being tipped off that there is either another way to draw the figure or that looking at the figure may be "deceptive." That is, just because something looks larger or smaller in the figure, it doesn't have to be. In this situation, if possible, quickly draw another possible figure that conforms to the information given.

Sample:

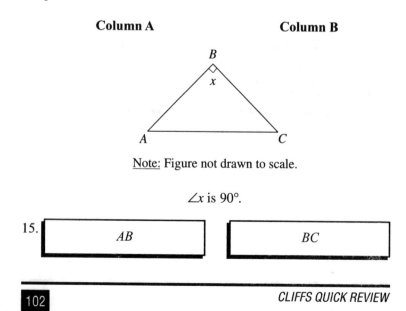

Column A   **Column B**

Note: Figure not drawn to scale.

$\angle x$ is 90°.

15. | AB | | BC |

From the figure, it appears that AB and BC are equal. But you could redraw the figure as follows.

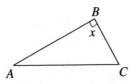

In this figure, AB is greater than BC, so the answer is (D). Since you got two different comparisons, no comparison can be determined from the information given.

Use familiar numbers. If you're given information that is unfamiliar to you and appears difficult to work with, change the number slightly (but remember your change) to a familiar number that is easier to work with.

Sample:

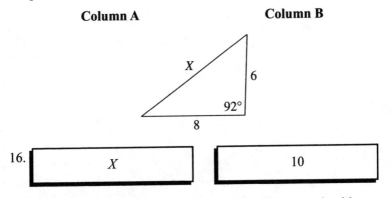

Column A   **Column B**

16. | X | | 10 |

Since 92°, as shown in the figure, is unfamiliar to work with, simply change it to 90° for now so that you can use the Pythagorean theorem.

$$a^2 + b^2 = c^2 \quad (c \text{ is always the longest side})$$

Solve for the longest side as follows.

$$6^2 + 8^2 = x^2$$
$$36 + 64 = x^2$$
$$100 = x^2$$
$$10 = x$$

But since you used 90° instead of 92°, you should realize that the side opposite the 92° will be slightly larger, or greater than 10. So the correct answer is (A), column A is greater.

If you notice the ratio of the sides of a 3 : 4 : 5 right triangle (in this case 6 : 8 : 10), you wouldn't have to use the Pythagorean theorem. This insight would make the comparison much faster.

GRID-IN QUESTIONS

The Basics of Grid-In Questions

The number of questions. You will have about 10 grid-in questions in a 25-problem math section. Typically, the grid-ins are questions 16 to 25.

The directions. The following questions require you to solve the problem and enter your answer by carefully marking the circles on the special grid.

A special note. Grid-in questions are very similar to multiple-choice questions except that you will solve the problem and enter your answer by carefully marking the circles on a special answer grid. You won't be selecting from a group of possible answers, so the answer that you grid in will give you either full credit or no credit. There is no partial credit, and there is no penalty for guessing on this section.

Marking in the grid (directions with analysis). The following questions require you to solve the problem and enter your answer by carefully marking the circles on the special grid. Examples of the appropriate way to mark the grid follow. (Comments in parentheses have been added to help you understand how to grid properly.)

Answer: 3.7

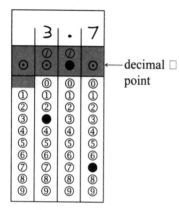

←—decimal point

(Notice that the decimal point is located in the shaded row, just above the numbers. Also notice that the answer has been written in above the gridding. You should always write in your answer, but the filled-in circles are most important because they are the ones scored.)

Answer: 1/2

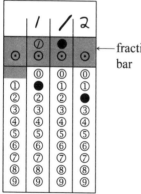

←—fraction bar

(Notice that the slash mark (/) indicates a fraction bar. This fraction bar is located in the shaded row and just above the decimal point in the two middle columns. Obviously, a fraction bar cannot be in the first or last column.)

Answer: $1\frac{1}{2}$

Do not grid in mixed numbers in the form of mixed numbers. **Always** change mixed numbers to improper fractions or decimals.

Change to 1.5 or **Change to 3/2**

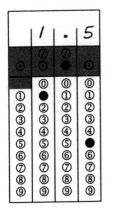 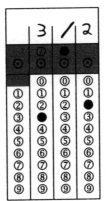

(Either an improper fraction or a decimal is acceptable. Never grid in a mixed number because it will always be mis-read. For example, $1\frac{1}{2}$ will be read by the computer doing the scoring as 11/2.)

Answer: 123

Space permitting, answers may start in any column. Each grid-in answer below is correct.

(You should try to grid your answers from right to left, learning to be consistent as you practice. But space permitting, you may start in any column.)

Note: Circles must be filled in correctly to receive credit. Mark only one circle in each column. No credit will be given if more than one circle in a column is marked. Example:

**Answer: 258
No credit!!!!**

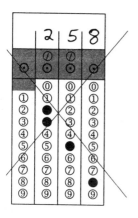

(Filling in more than one circle in a column is equivalent to selecting more than one answer in multiple choice. This type of answer fill-in will never receive any credit. Be careful to avoid this mistake.)

Answer: 8/9

Accuracy of decimals: Always enter the most accurate decimal value that the grid will accommodate. For example: An answer such as .8888 . . . can be gridded as .888 or .889. Gridding this value as .8, .88, or .89 is considered inaccurate and therefore **not acceptable.** The acceptable grid-ins of 8/9 are

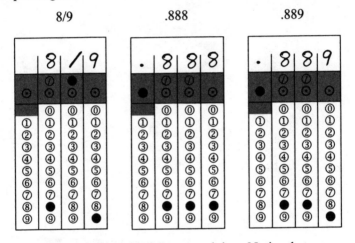

(Review "accuracy of decimals" a second time. Notice that you must be as accurate as the grid allows.)

Be sure to write your answers in the boxes at the top of the circles before doing your gridding. Although writing out the answers above the columns is not required, it is very important to ensure accuracy. Even though some problems may have more than one correct answer, grid only **one answer.** Grid-in questions contain no negative answers.

Fractions can be reduced to lowest terms, but it is not required as long as they will fit in the grid. You are not required to grid a zero before a fraction. For example, either .2 or 0.2 is acceptable. If your answer is zero, you are required only to grid a zero in one column. **Important:** If you decide to change an answer, be sure to erase the old gridded answer completely.)

Try a few. The following few practice grids will help you become familiar with the gridding process. Properly filled-in grids are given following the practice. Hand write and grid in the answers given.

Answer: 685   **Answer: 1,542**   **Answer: 4.5**

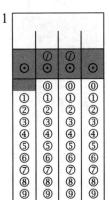   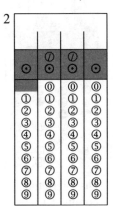   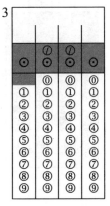

Answer: $3\frac{1}{4}$ **Answer: .222 . . .**   **Answer: .666 . . .**

Filled-in grids:

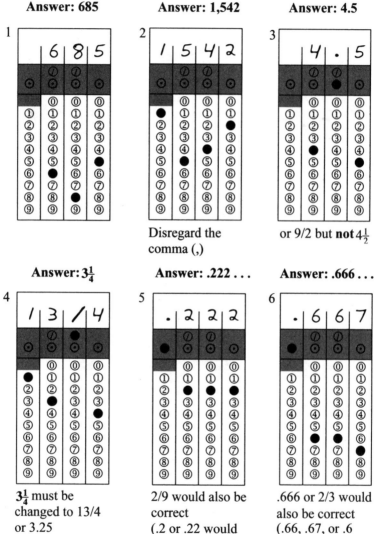

Answer: 685

Answer: 1,542

Disregard the comma (,)

Answer: 4.5

or 9/2 but **not** $4\frac{1}{2}$

Answer: $3\frac{1}{4}$

$3\frac{1}{4}$ must be changed to 13/4 or 3.25

Answer: .222 . . .

2/9 would also be correct
(.2 or .22 would **not** be correct)

Answer: .666 . . .

.666 or 2/3 would also be correct
(.66, .67, or .6 would **not** be correct)

The Questions and Key Strategies for Grid-Ins

General problem-solving strategies. The following strategies, described and suggested in the multiple-choice section, will also work on grid-in questions.

- Underline or circle what you're looking for.
- Simplify the problem.
- Work forward.
- Plug in simple numbers.
- Pull out information.
- Mark in, or fill in, the diagram.
- If no diagram is given, draw one.
- Note that some diagrams are not drawn to scale.
- Use 10 or 100.
- Be reasonable.

Specific strategies for grid-ins.

- Realize there is no penalty for guessing on grid-in questions.
- Know the grid-in rules and procedures.
- Write in your answer at the top, but understand that only the actual grid-in is scored.
- Change mixed numbers to improper fractions.
- Understand that fraction and decimal forms are acceptable.
- Grid in only one answer, even if more than one is possible.
- Make sure you answer the question in the units asked for.
- Use your calculator to your advantage.
- Check your answer, if time permits.

Realize there is no penalty for guessing on grid-in questions. Since you don't have the advantage of choosing from a group of answer choices, no points are deducted for incorrect answers in this section. That is, there is no penalty for guessing or attempting a grid-in. So even though it may be difficult to get a correct answer by simply writing in a wild guess, you shouldn't be afraid to fill in an answer on problems you can't solve—even if you think it's wrong.

Know the grid-in rules and procedures. Review the grid-in information given above carefully. Practice gridding in some answers. Become comfortable with the grid-in process.

Write in your answer at the top, but understand that only the actual grid-in is scored. Your gridding must be accurate. To help you grid accurately, always carefully write your answer in at the top part of the grid. Even though the written-in part isn't scored, it can be very helpful.

Change mixed numbers to improper fractions. Answers that are mixed numbers, such as $1\frac{1}{2}$ must be changed to improper fractions ($4\frac{1}{2} = 9/2$) or decimals ($4\frac{1}{2} = 4.5$) before being gridded. Mixed numbers cannot be gridded; the scoring system cannot distinguish between 4 1/2 and 41/2.

Understand that fraction and decimal forms are acceptable.

Sample:

1. Let $m\#n$ be defined as $m - \left(\frac{1}{2}\right)n$. What is the value of $4\#3$?

First underline or circle "value of 4#3." This problem involves a made-up operation, or "false operation." The "#" is the false-operation sign and must be defined. Notice how it is defined.

$$m\#n \text{ is defined as } m - \left(\tfrac{1}{2}\right)n$$

Now simply substitute 4 for m and 3 for n to get a value.

$$m - \left(\tfrac{1}{2}\right)n = 4 - \left(\tfrac{1}{2}\right)3$$
$$= 4 - 1\tfrac{1}{2}$$
$$= 2\tfrac{1}{2}$$

But you can't grid $2\tfrac{1}{2}$, so you must change it to *either* 5/2 or 2.5. Now you can fill in the top and grid in the answer. Your grid-in would look like this.

Grid in only one answer, even if more than one is possible. In some questions, more than one answer is possible. You need to grid in only one of the possible answers; don't grid in more than one.

Sample:

1. If x and y are positive integers and $x + y > 10$, what is a possible value of x if $y > 5$?

First underline or circle the words "possible value of x." Since $y > 5$, try plugging in 6 for y, and see what you get.

$$x + 6 > 10$$

Subtracting 6 from each side leaves

$$
\begin{array}{r}
x + 6 > 10 \\
-6 \;\; -6 \\
\hline
x \quad > \;\; 4
\end{array}
$$

So, *in this case*, x is any integer greater than 4—that is, 5, 6, 7, 8, ... (If you assign a larger number to y, you'll get other possibilities for x.)

Now simply write in one answer, say 5, and then carefully mark it in the grid. Don't put in more than one possibility. Your grid could look like this.

Make sure you answer the question in the units asked for. Be sure to underline or circle what the question is asking, paying special attention to the units.

Sample:

Lawns in Hillcrest Village		
Street name	**Number of lawns**	**Mowing time per lawn**
Pine	3	25 minutes
Tamarind	7	30 minutes
Randall	9	35 minutes
Palmetto	12	40 minutes

3. How many hours will it take to mow all of the lawns listed in the chart above?

   First underline or circle "how many hours" and "all of the lawns." Next set up the information as follows and multiply (use your calculator if you wish).

$$3 \times 25 = 75$$
$$7 \times 30 = 210$$
$$9 \times 35 = 315$$
$$12 \times 40 = 480$$

   Now total the minutes, and you get 1,080 minutes. But the question asks for *hours,* so divide 1,080 by 60 (use your calculator if you wish), and you get 18 *hours.* (Sometimes the units will be underlined in the question.) Your grid-in would look like the one that follows.

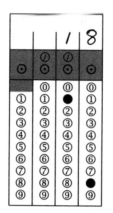

Use your calculator to your advantage. Since no answer choices are given, you'll have to actually work out each answer. Using your calculator on some problems in this section can enhance the speed and accuracy of your work.

Sample:

4. What is $\left(\frac{4}{5}\right)\%$ of 655?

   The correct answer is 5.24. You could solve as follows.

$$\left(\tfrac{4}{5}\right)\% \text{ of } 655 = (.80\%)(655)$$
$$= (.0080)(655)$$
$$= 5.24$$

Your calculator would be very helpful in this problem. Your grid-in would look like this.

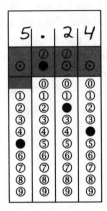

Check your answer, if time permits. Since no answer choices are given, you may want to check your answer, if time permits. Your calculator can be helpful here.

Sample:

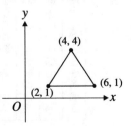

5. What is the area of the triangle in the figure above?

First underline or circle "area of the triangle." The formula for the area of a triangle is $\frac{1}{2} \times$ base $\times$ height. Next determine the length of the base. Since the coordinates of the base are (2, 1) and (6, 1), simply subtract the x coordinates, $6 - 2$, and you can see that the base is 4. Since the coordinates of the top of the triangle are (4, 4) and those of the base are (2, 1) and (6, 1), the height can be found by subtracting the y coordinates, $4 - 1$, giving you 3. Using the area formula,

$$\text{area} = \left(\tfrac{1}{2}\right)bh$$
$$= \left(\tfrac{1}{2}\right)(4)(3)$$
$$= 2(3)$$
$$= 6$$

The correct answer is 6. Now, if time permits, go back and check your steps and calculations. Your grid-in would look like this.

CHARTS AND GRAPHS

The Basics of Charts and Graphs

The number of questions. The Mathematical Reasoning sections of the SAT I include some questions about charts and graphs. You'll usually have one or two questions for each chart or graph. The number of charts or graphs in a section usually range between none and three.

What you should know. You should know how to

- read and understand information given
- calculate, analyze, and apply information given
- spot trends and patterns
- predict future trends and patterns

The Key Strategies for Charts and Graphs

- Focus on understanding what information is given.
- Don't memorize the information; refer to the chart or graph.
- Review additional information given (headings, scale factors, legends, and so forth).
- Read the question and the answer choices, focusing on key words.
- Look for obvious large changes (high points, low points, trends, and so forth).

Charts

Charts are often used to give an organized picture of information or data. Know *what information is given* in the chart. Column headings, titles, and line items are important information. Focus on these items, since they give the numbers meaning.

A chart and sample questions:

Questions 1-2 are based on the following chart, which shows the amount of money collected during a school's magazine sale.

Magazine Sale Income				
Cost of magazine	$10	$12	$15	$19
Number sold	6	3	4	2

1. Which of the following is the mode of the cost of the magazines sold during the magazine sale?
   (A) $10   (B) $11   (C) $12   (D) $15   (E) $19

   The correct answer is (A). The mode is the cost that appears the most. Six $10 magazines were sold.

2. If the magazine company gives the school 50% of the magazine sale income, how much money does the school get?
   (A) $54   (B) $56   (C) $92   (D) $97   (E) $194

   The correct answer is (D) $97. First multiply out the information as follows.

   $$6 \times 10 = 60$$
   $$3 \times 12 = 36$$
   $$4 \times 15 = 60$$
   $$2 \times 19 = 38$$

Next, total the right column to get the total amount of money, which is $194. Now take 50% of $194, which is $97.

Graphs

Information is usually displayed in three basic types of graphs.

- bar graphs
- line graphs
- circle graphs (pie charts)

Bar graphs. Bar graphs display information as separate bars or columns. Some bar graphs list numbers along one edge and places, dates, people, or other items along another edge. Always determine the relationship between the columns in a bar graph.

A bar graph and sample questions:

Questions 3-4 are based on the following graph.

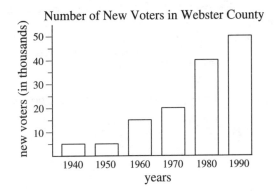

3. In 1977, the number of new voters was approximately
   (A) 20,000
   (B) 23,000
   (C) 30,000
   (D) 37,000
   (E) It cannot be determined from the information given.

The correct answer is (E). It's important to understand what the graph is telling you and what information you can infer from it. From this graph, you can't figure out the number of new voters in 1977, even though you know the number of voters in 1970 and the number in 1980.

4. From the graph above, between which of the following two years was there the greatest percent increase in voter registration?
   (A) 1940 and 1950
   (B) 1950 and 1960
   (C) 1960 and 1970
   (D) 1970 and 1980
   (E) 1980 and 1990

The correct answer is (B). The percent increase is figured as follows.

$$\frac{\text{change}}{\text{starting point}} \times 100 = \text{percent increase}$$

Choice (A): Between 1940 and 1950, there is no increase at all.

Choice (B):

$$\frac{15-5}{5} \times 100 = \frac{10}{5} \times 100$$
$$= 2 \times 100$$
$$= 200\%$$

Choice (C): From the graph, you can see that this increase is very small.

Choice (D):

$$\frac{40-20}{20} \times 100 = \frac{20}{20} \times 100$$
$$= 1 \times 100$$
$$= 100\%$$

Choice (E):

$$\frac{50-40}{40} \times 100 = \frac{10}{40} \times 100$$
$$= \frac{1}{4} \times 100$$
$$= .25 \times 100$$
$$= 25\%$$

Notice that the *greatest increase* is not necessarily the *greatest percent increase.*

Line graphs. Line graphs show data as points on a grid. These points are then connected to make the relationship among dates, times, numbers, years, items, and so forth, more evident. Pay special attention to the slopes of the lines that connect the points, as they will help you spot increases and decreases. The steeper the slope upward to the right, the greater the increase. The steeper the slope downward to the right, the greater the decrease. Line graphs can show trends, or changes, in data over a period of time.

A line graph and sample questions:

Questions 5-6 are based on the following graph.

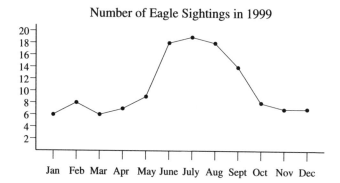

Number of Eagle Sightings in 1999

5. Between which of the following months was there the greatest decrease in the number of eagle sightings?
   (A) January and February
   (B) March and April
   (C) June and July
   (D) September and October
   (E) November and December

The correct answer is (D). The steepest slope downward is the greatest decrease.

6. Which of the following is a reasonable prediction that can be made for the year 2000 from the graph?

   (A) More eagles will be sighted early in the year than late in the year.

   (B) The greatest number of eagle sightings will be during the summer months.

   (C) The number of eagle sightings toward the end of the year will be fewer than those toward the end of 1999.

   (D) The fewest number of eagle sightings will occur between February and April.

   (E) The number of eagle sightings will increase toward the end of the year.

The correct answer is (B). From the line graph, it appears that the number of sightings is greatest during June, July, and August, which could reasonably lead you to predict that the greatest number of sightings in 2000 will also occur during the summer months. The graph gives no information that would lead to the predictions in the other choices.

Circle graphs. A circle graph, also referred to as a pie chart, shows the relationship between the whole circle (100%) and various pieces, or slices, that represent portions of that 100%. The higher the percentage, the larger the slice.

A circle graph and sample questions:

Questions 7-8 are based on the following circle graph.

How Oscar Spends His 24-Hour Day

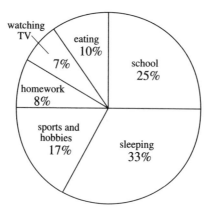

7. According to the graph, how many hours does Oscar spend at school?

(A) 3   (B) 4   (C) 5   (D) 6   (E) 8

The correct answer is (D). Since 25% of Oscar's time is spent at school, simply multiply 25% times 24.

$$.25 \times 24 = 6$$

or change 25% to $\frac{1}{4}$ and multiply times 24

$$\frac{1}{4} \times 24^6 = 6$$

8. From the circle graph, approximately how many more hours will Oscar spend sleeping than doing homework during a five-day period?

   (A) 6   (B) 10   (C) 12   (D) 20   (E) 30

   The correct answer is (E). Sleeping is 33% of 24, which is about one third of 24, or 8 hours. Homework is 8% of 24, or $.08 \times 24$, which is about 2 hours. The difference between 8 hours and 2 hours is 6 hours. Now, multiplying by 5 (for the five-day period),

   $$6 \text{ hours} \times 5 = 30 \text{ hours}$$

Coordinate graphs (x-y graphs). A coordinate graph is formed by two perpendicular number lines. These lines are called coordinate axes. The horizontal axis is called the x-axis or the abscissa. The vertical line is called the y-axis or the ordinate. The point at which the two lines intersect is called the origin and is represented by the coordinates (0, 0), often marked simply O.

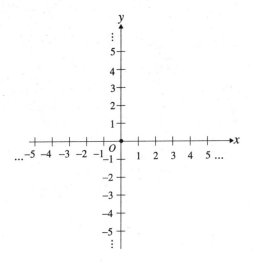

Each point on a coordinate graph is located by an ordered pair of numbers called coordinates. Notice the placement of points on the graph below and the coordinates, or ordered pairs, that show their location. Numbers are not usually given on the x and y axes. Depending on the type of problem involved, the tick marks may be given along with the coordinates, but often only the coordinates are given.

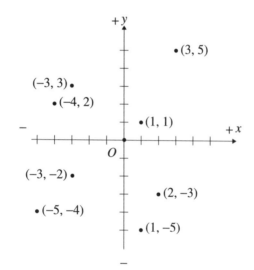

Also notice that on the x-axis the numbers to the right of 0 are positive and to the left of 0 are negative. On the y-axis, numbers above 0 are positive and numbers below 0 are negative. The first number in the ordered pair is called the x-coordinate and shows how far to the right or left of 0 the point is. The second number is called the y-coordinate and shows how far up or down the point is from 0. The coordinates, or ordered pairs, are shown as (x, y). The order of these numbers is very important, as the point $(3, 2)$ is different from the point $(2, 3)$. Also, don't combine the ordered pair of numbers, as they refer to different directions.

The coordinate graph is divided into four quarters called quadrants. These quadrants are labeled as follows.

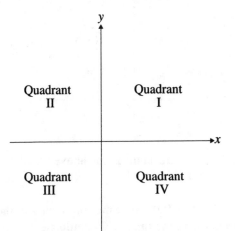

You can see that

- In quadrant I, x is always positive and y is always positive.
- In quadrant II, x is always negative and y is always positive.
- In quadrant III, x is always negative and y is always negative.
- In quadrant IV, x is always positive and y is always negative.

Coordinate graphs and sample questions:

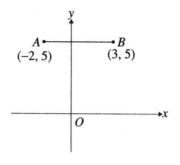

9. What is the length of *AB* in the graph above?
   (A) 3   (B) 4   (C) $4\frac{1}{2}$ (D) 5   (E) $5\frac{1}{2}$

   The correct answer is (D). Since the coordinates of the points
   are (–2, 5) and (3, 5), the first, or *x*, coordinate will tip you off
   to the distance of each point from the *y*-axis. The distance to
   point *B* from the *y*-axis is 3, and the distance to point *A* from the
   y-axis is 2 (–2 is 2 in the negative direction). So $3 + 2$ gives a
   length of 5.

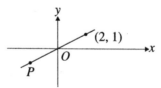

10. In the coordinate graph above, if the line passes through the ori-
    gin, which of the following could be the coordinates of point *P*?
    (A) (1, 1)
    (B) (–1, 0)
    (C) (–1, 1)
    (D) (–2, 0)
    (E) (–2, –1)

The correct answer is (E). In this particular problem only choice (E) is reasonable. Since point *P* is in the third quadrant, both coordinates must be negative. From the slope of the line you could see that (–2,–1) would lie on it.

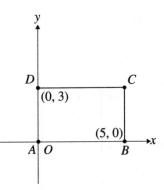

11. What is the area of rectangle *ABCD* in the graph above?
    (A) 3   (B) 5   (C) 8   (D) 15   (E) 16

The correct answer is (D). The formula for the area of a rectangle is base × height. Since point *A* is at (0, 0) and point *B* is at (5, 0), the base is 5. Since point *D* is at (0, 3), the height is 3, so the area is $5 \times 3 = 15$.

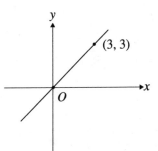

12. What is the slope of the line that passes through the origin (0, 0) and (3, 3) in the graph above?
    (A) 0   (B) 1   (C) 2   (D) 3   (E) 6

The correct answer is (B). The slope is the rise/run, or the change in y over the change in x. From the graph, you can see that if the line goes up 3, it also goes 3 to the right. $\frac{3}{3} = 1$. You could also use the slope formula.

$$\text{slope} = \frac{(y_2 - y_1)}{(x_2 - x_1)} = \frac{3-0}{3-0} = \frac{3}{3} = 1$$

So the slope is 1.

Puzzle Types

You may be asked to solve or fill in a puzzle—that is, to replace blank spaces or letters with the right number. Approaching these problems part by part and using common sense is helpful.

Sample:

10	y	z
x	v	9
6	w	4

1. If each row, column, and diagonal in the chart totals 21, then what is the value of $x + y + z$?
   (A) 16   (B) 21   (C) 37   (D) 42   (E) 44

   The correct answer is (A). You should first use some logic to fill in the chart. Since the total of each row, column, and diagonal is 21, the x must be 5 because the other two numbers in the column total 16. The two numbers in the right column total 13, so z must be 8. The first row now has 10 and 8, so y must be 3 to total 21.

   The chart would look like this.

10	$y = 3$	$z = 8$
$x = 5$	v	9
6	w	4

   So the total of $x + y + z$ is $5 + 3 + 8 = 16$.

Another sample:

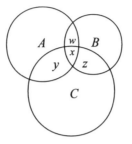

2. In the diagram above, circle A is composed of multiples of 3, circle B is composed of multiples of 5, and circle C is composed of multiples of 2. If w, x, y, and z represent numbers that are in the intersections as shown above, which of the following is the least possible value of the product of $wxyz$?

    (A)   2,700
    (B)   5,400
    (C)   8,100
    (D) 27,000
    (E) 54,000

The correct answer is (D). Since the question asks for the least possible value, you should select the smallest multiples of each number and fill in the diagram as follows.

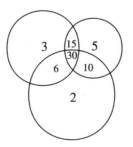

Now use your calculator to multiply.

$$15 \times 30 \times 6 \times 10 = 27,000$$

Another sample:

$$
\begin{array}{r}
Y\ 4 \\
5\ X \\
+\ 1\ 6\ 3 \\
\hline
Y\ 4\ 1
\end{array}
$$

3. In the addition problem above, X and Y stand for different digits in the correctly worked problem. What is the value of $X + Y$?
   (A) 2   (B) 4   (C) 6   (D) 8   (E) 10

   The correct answer is (C). Since the ones column already has a total of 7 $(3 + 4)$, then X must equal 4 because the total in that column ends in 1 (and 11 is the only possibility). Now carrying the 1 into the tens column plus the 6 and 5 (already there) gives 12. But the tens place in the answer must be 4, so Y must be 2, leaving 14. This is consistent because 1 is carried into the hundreds place plus the 1 already there, which gives 2 for Y in the hundreds column in the answer. So $X = 4$ and $Y = 2$. Therefore, $X + Y = 6$.

Spatials

Some problems test your ability to visualize and analyze three-dimensional shapes, movements, or paper folds. Marking or focusing on key spots can be helpful.

Sample:

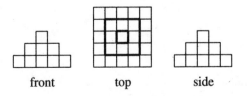

front   top   side

4. The figure above shows three different views of a solid that is constructed from cubes. Each cube is the same size and has a volume of one cubic inch. How many cubes are needed to build the solid?

(A) 35   (B) 26   (C) 25   (D) 17   (E) 9

The correct answer is (A). First you should carefully review each view of the solid. You'll see that the bottom layer is made up of 25 cubes (5×5). The next layer is made up of 9 cubes (3×3). And the top is one cube. So the total number of cubes needed to build the solid is

$$25 + 9 + 1 = 35$$

Another sample:

5. Which of the following could be folded along the dotted lines to form a rectangular solid?

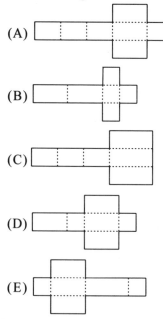

(A)

(B)

(C)

(D)

(E)

The correct answer is (D). You should focus (or put an X) on the piece of each diagram that has the most parts connected to it. Then mentally fold the rest of the sides around the piece you marked, making it easier for you to spot the answer that will form a rectangular solid.

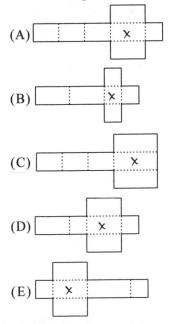

Notice that choice (D) folds perfectly into a rectangular solid.

Another sample:

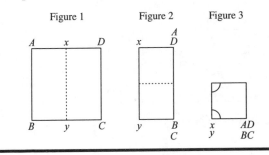

6. In Figure 1 above, a square piece of paper is folded along dotted line xy so that A is on top of D and B is on top of C (Figure 2). The paper is then folded again so that x is on top of y and AD is on top of BC (Figure 3). Two corners are cut in a circular fashion out of the folded paper as shown in Figure 3. If the paper is unfolded, which of the following could be the result?

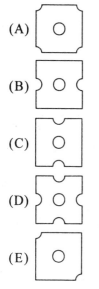

(A)

(B)

(C)

(D)

(E)

The correct answer is (C). The best way to understand what will happen is to cut a square sheet of paper with some scissors following the directions given above. On your exam, however, you should mark the figures, starting with Figure 3 and working back.

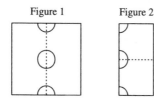

Figure 1   Figure 2   Figure 3

Notice where the holes end up.

Special Symbols

In some problems, you may be given symbols that you're unfamiliar with. Don't let these "special symbols" confuse or alarm you. Even though these symbols may look unusual, they typically represent an operation or combination of operations that you are familiar with. These operations are sometimes referred to as "false operations." Read carefully to see how the special symbol is defined. This definition is the key to solving the problem.

Sample:

7. Let # be defined for all nonzero integers x and y such that

$$x \# y = \frac{x+y}{xy}$$

What is the value of 5#3?
(A) 1   (B) $\frac{8}{3}$ (C) $\frac{5}{3}$ (D) $\frac{8}{15}$ (E) $\frac{2}{15}$

The correct answer is (D). Simply replace x with 5 and y with 3 in the equation given.

$$x \# y = \frac{x+y}{xy}$$

$$5 \# 3 = \frac{5+3}{(5)(3)}$$

$$= \frac{8}{15}$$

Another sample:

8. If $\begin{array}{|c|c|} \hline w & x \\ \hline y & z \\ \hline \end{array} = wy + xz$, then what is the value of $\begin{array}{|c|c|} \hline 2 & 3 \\ \hline 4 & 5 \\ \hline \end{array}$?

(A) 5   (B) 14   (C) 23   (D) 26   (E) 120

The correct answer is (C). Simply replacing w with 2, x with 3, y with 4, and z with 5 gives

$$wy + xz = 2(4) + 3(5)$$
$$= 8 + 15$$
$$= 23$$

Sequences

You may be asked to identify a sequence of numbers or figures. If numbers are given, look for a pattern (increasing, decreasing, odd numbers, even numbers, and so forth).

Sample:

$$3, 5, 9, 17, 33, \ldots$$

9. Which of the following is the next number in the series given above?
   (A) 6   (B) 32   (C) 33   (D) 50   (E) 65

The correct answer is (E). Notice that the pattern here is based on powers of 2.

Therefore, the answer is 65.

$$33 + 32 = 65$$

PRACTICE TEST

Note: The problems in the following practice test are not taken from an actual SAT I, as those problems are copyrighted.

ANSWER SHEET FOR THE PRACTICE TEST
(Remove This Sheet and Use It to Mark Your Answers)

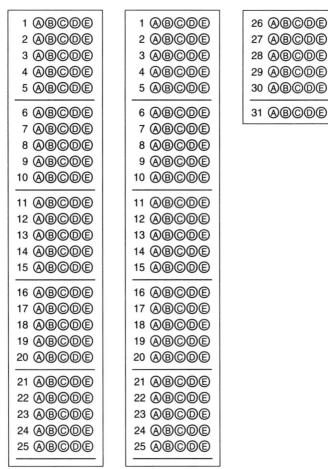

SECTION 1

1 Ⓐ Ⓑ Ⓒ Ⓓ Ⓔ
2 Ⓐ Ⓑ Ⓒ Ⓓ Ⓔ
3 Ⓐ Ⓑ Ⓒ Ⓓ Ⓔ
4 Ⓐ Ⓑ Ⓒ Ⓓ Ⓔ
5 Ⓐ Ⓑ Ⓒ Ⓓ Ⓔ

6 Ⓐ Ⓑ Ⓒ Ⓓ Ⓔ
7 Ⓐ Ⓑ Ⓒ Ⓓ Ⓔ
8 Ⓐ Ⓑ Ⓒ Ⓓ Ⓔ
9 Ⓐ Ⓑ Ⓒ Ⓓ Ⓔ
10 Ⓐ Ⓑ Ⓒ Ⓓ Ⓔ

11 Ⓐ Ⓑ Ⓒ Ⓓ Ⓔ
12 Ⓐ Ⓑ Ⓒ Ⓓ Ⓔ
13 Ⓐ Ⓑ Ⓒ Ⓓ Ⓔ
14 Ⓐ Ⓑ Ⓒ Ⓓ Ⓔ
15 Ⓐ Ⓑ Ⓒ Ⓓ Ⓔ

16 Ⓐ Ⓑ Ⓒ Ⓓ Ⓔ
17 Ⓐ Ⓑ Ⓒ Ⓓ Ⓔ
18 Ⓐ Ⓑ Ⓒ Ⓓ Ⓔ
19 Ⓐ Ⓑ Ⓒ Ⓓ Ⓔ
20 Ⓐ Ⓑ Ⓒ Ⓓ Ⓔ

21 Ⓐ Ⓑ Ⓒ Ⓓ Ⓔ
22 Ⓐ Ⓑ Ⓒ Ⓓ Ⓔ
23 Ⓐ Ⓑ Ⓒ Ⓓ Ⓔ
24 Ⓐ Ⓑ Ⓒ Ⓓ Ⓔ
25 Ⓐ Ⓑ Ⓒ Ⓓ Ⓔ

SECTION 2

1 Ⓐ Ⓑ Ⓒ Ⓓ Ⓔ
2 Ⓐ Ⓑ Ⓒ Ⓓ Ⓔ
3 Ⓐ Ⓑ Ⓒ Ⓓ Ⓔ
4 Ⓐ Ⓑ Ⓒ Ⓓ Ⓔ
5 Ⓐ Ⓑ Ⓒ Ⓓ Ⓔ

6 Ⓐ Ⓑ Ⓒ Ⓓ Ⓔ
7 Ⓐ Ⓑ Ⓒ Ⓓ Ⓔ
8 Ⓐ Ⓑ Ⓒ Ⓓ Ⓔ
9 Ⓐ Ⓑ Ⓒ Ⓓ Ⓔ
10 Ⓐ Ⓑ Ⓒ Ⓓ Ⓔ

11 Ⓐ Ⓑ Ⓒ Ⓓ Ⓔ
12 Ⓐ Ⓑ Ⓒ Ⓓ Ⓔ
13 Ⓐ Ⓑ Ⓒ Ⓓ Ⓔ
14 Ⓐ Ⓑ Ⓒ Ⓓ Ⓔ
15 Ⓐ Ⓑ Ⓒ Ⓓ Ⓔ

16 Ⓐ Ⓑ Ⓒ Ⓓ Ⓔ
17 Ⓐ Ⓑ Ⓒ Ⓓ Ⓔ
18 Ⓐ Ⓑ Ⓒ Ⓓ Ⓔ
19 Ⓐ Ⓑ Ⓒ Ⓓ Ⓔ
20 Ⓐ Ⓑ Ⓒ Ⓓ Ⓔ

21 Ⓐ Ⓑ Ⓒ Ⓓ Ⓔ
22 Ⓐ Ⓑ Ⓒ Ⓓ Ⓔ
23 Ⓐ Ⓑ Ⓒ Ⓓ Ⓔ
24 Ⓐ Ⓑ Ⓒ Ⓓ Ⓔ
25 Ⓐ Ⓑ Ⓒ Ⓓ Ⓔ

SECTION 3

26 Ⓐ Ⓑ Ⓒ Ⓓ Ⓔ
27 Ⓐ Ⓑ Ⓒ Ⓓ Ⓔ
28 Ⓐ Ⓑ Ⓒ Ⓓ Ⓔ
29 Ⓐ Ⓑ Ⓒ Ⓓ Ⓔ
30 Ⓐ Ⓑ Ⓒ Ⓓ Ⓔ

31 Ⓐ Ⓑ Ⓒ Ⓓ Ⓔ

---CUT HERE---

ANSWER SHEET FOR THE PRACTICE TEST
(Remove This Sheet and Use It to Mark Your Answers)

SECTION 3

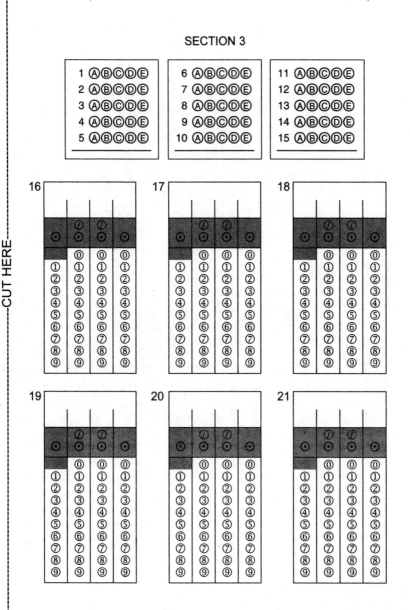

SECTION 3, continued

22

23

24

25

CUT HERE

ANSWER SHEET FOR THE PRACTICE TEST
(Remove This Sheet and Use It to Mark Your Answers)

SECTION 4

1 Ⓐ Ⓑ Ⓒ Ⓓ Ⓔ
2 Ⓐ Ⓑ Ⓒ Ⓓ Ⓔ
3 Ⓐ Ⓑ Ⓒ Ⓓ Ⓔ
4 Ⓐ Ⓑ Ⓒ Ⓓ Ⓔ
5 Ⓐ Ⓑ Ⓒ Ⓓ Ⓔ

6 Ⓐ Ⓑ Ⓒ Ⓓ Ⓔ
7 Ⓐ Ⓑ Ⓒ Ⓓ Ⓔ
8 Ⓐ Ⓑ Ⓒ Ⓓ Ⓔ
9 Ⓐ Ⓑ Ⓒ Ⓓ Ⓔ
10 Ⓐ Ⓑ Ⓒ Ⓓ Ⓔ

11 Ⓐ Ⓑ Ⓒ Ⓓ Ⓔ
12 Ⓐ Ⓑ Ⓒ Ⓓ Ⓔ
13 Ⓐ Ⓑ Ⓒ Ⓓ Ⓔ
14 Ⓐ Ⓑ Ⓒ Ⓓ Ⓔ
15 Ⓐ Ⓑ Ⓒ Ⓓ Ⓔ

16 Ⓐ Ⓑ Ⓒ Ⓓ Ⓔ
17 Ⓐ Ⓑ Ⓒ Ⓓ Ⓔ
18 Ⓐ Ⓑ Ⓒ Ⓓ Ⓔ
19 Ⓐ Ⓑ Ⓒ Ⓓ Ⓔ
20 Ⓐ Ⓑ Ⓒ Ⓓ Ⓔ

21 Ⓐ Ⓑ Ⓒ Ⓓ Ⓔ
22 Ⓐ Ⓑ Ⓒ Ⓓ Ⓔ
23 Ⓐ Ⓑ Ⓒ Ⓓ Ⓔ
24 Ⓐ Ⓑ Ⓒ Ⓓ Ⓔ
25 Ⓐ Ⓑ Ⓒ Ⓓ Ⓔ

26 Ⓐ Ⓑ Ⓒ Ⓓ Ⓔ
27 Ⓐ Ⓑ Ⓒ Ⓓ Ⓔ
28 Ⓐ Ⓑ Ⓒ Ⓓ Ⓔ
29 Ⓐ Ⓑ Ⓒ Ⓓ Ⓔ
30 Ⓐ Ⓑ Ⓒ Ⓓ Ⓔ

31 Ⓐ Ⓑ Ⓒ Ⓓ Ⓔ
32 Ⓐ Ⓑ Ⓒ Ⓓ Ⓔ
33 Ⓐ Ⓑ Ⓒ Ⓓ Ⓔ
34 Ⓐ Ⓑ Ⓒ Ⓓ Ⓔ
35 Ⓐ Ⓑ Ⓒ Ⓓ Ⓔ

SECTION 5

1 Ⓐ Ⓑ Ⓒ Ⓓ Ⓔ
2 Ⓐ Ⓑ Ⓒ Ⓓ Ⓔ
3 Ⓐ Ⓑ Ⓒ Ⓓ Ⓔ
4 Ⓐ Ⓑ Ⓒ Ⓓ Ⓔ
5 Ⓐ Ⓑ Ⓒ Ⓓ Ⓔ

6 Ⓐ Ⓑ Ⓒ Ⓓ Ⓔ
7 Ⓐ Ⓑ Ⓒ Ⓓ Ⓔ
8 Ⓐ Ⓑ Ⓒ Ⓓ Ⓔ
9 Ⓐ Ⓑ Ⓒ Ⓓ Ⓔ
10 Ⓐ Ⓑ Ⓒ Ⓓ Ⓔ

CUT HERE

ANSWER SHEET FOR THE PRACTICE TEST
(Remove This Sheet and Use It to Mark Your Answers)

SECTION 6

1 Ⓐ Ⓑ Ⓒ Ⓓ Ⓔ
2 Ⓐ Ⓑ Ⓒ Ⓓ Ⓔ
3 Ⓐ Ⓑ Ⓒ Ⓓ Ⓔ
4 Ⓐ Ⓑ Ⓒ Ⓓ Ⓔ
5 Ⓐ Ⓑ Ⓒ Ⓓ Ⓔ

6 Ⓐ Ⓑ Ⓒ Ⓓ Ⓔ
7 Ⓐ Ⓑ Ⓒ Ⓓ Ⓔ
8 Ⓐ Ⓑ Ⓒ Ⓓ Ⓔ
9 Ⓐ Ⓑ Ⓒ Ⓓ Ⓔ
10 Ⓐ Ⓑ Ⓒ Ⓓ Ⓔ

11 Ⓐ Ⓑ Ⓒ Ⓓ Ⓔ
12 Ⓐ Ⓑ Ⓒ Ⓓ Ⓔ
13 Ⓐ Ⓑ Ⓒ Ⓓ Ⓔ
14 Ⓐ Ⓑ Ⓒ Ⓓ Ⓔ
15 Ⓐ Ⓑ Ⓒ Ⓓ Ⓔ

SECTION 7

1 Ⓐ Ⓑ Ⓒ Ⓓ Ⓔ
2 Ⓐ Ⓑ Ⓒ Ⓓ Ⓔ
3 Ⓐ Ⓑ Ⓒ Ⓓ Ⓔ
4 Ⓐ Ⓑ Ⓒ Ⓓ Ⓔ
5 Ⓐ Ⓑ Ⓒ Ⓓ Ⓔ

6 Ⓐ Ⓑ Ⓒ Ⓓ Ⓔ
7 Ⓐ Ⓑ Ⓒ Ⓓ Ⓔ
8 Ⓐ Ⓑ Ⓒ Ⓓ Ⓔ
9 Ⓐ Ⓑ Ⓒ Ⓓ Ⓔ
10 Ⓐ Ⓑ Ⓒ Ⓓ Ⓔ

11 Ⓐ Ⓑ Ⓒ Ⓓ Ⓔ
12 Ⓐ Ⓑ Ⓒ Ⓓ Ⓔ
13 Ⓐ Ⓑ Ⓒ Ⓓ Ⓔ
14 Ⓐ Ⓑ Ⓒ Ⓓ Ⓔ
15 Ⓐ Ⓑ Ⓒ Ⓓ Ⓔ

16 Ⓐ Ⓑ Ⓒ Ⓓ Ⓔ
17 Ⓐ Ⓑ Ⓒ Ⓓ Ⓔ
18 Ⓐ Ⓑ Ⓒ Ⓓ Ⓔ
19 Ⓐ Ⓑ Ⓒ Ⓓ Ⓔ
20 Ⓐ Ⓑ Ⓒ Ⓓ Ⓔ

21 Ⓐ Ⓑ Ⓒ Ⓓ Ⓔ
22 Ⓐ Ⓑ Ⓒ Ⓓ Ⓔ
23 Ⓐ Ⓑ Ⓒ Ⓓ Ⓔ
24 Ⓐ Ⓑ Ⓒ Ⓓ Ⓔ
25 Ⓐ Ⓑ Ⓒ Ⓓ Ⓔ

CUT HERE

CLIFFS QUICK REVIEW

Time: 30 Minutes
25 Questions

DIRECTIONS

Solve each problem in this section by using the information given and your own mathematical calculations, insights, and problem-solving skills. Then select the one correct answer of the five choices given and mark the corresponding circle on your answer sheet. Use the available space on the page for your scratch work.

Notes

(1) All numbers used are real numbers.
(2) Calculators may be used.
(3) Some problems may be accompanied by figures or diagrams. These figures are drawn as accurately as possible except when it is stated in a specific problem that a figure is not drawn to scale. The figures and diagrams are meant to provide information useful in solving the problem or problems. Unless otherwise stated, all figures and diagrams lie in a plane.

Data That May Be Used for Reference

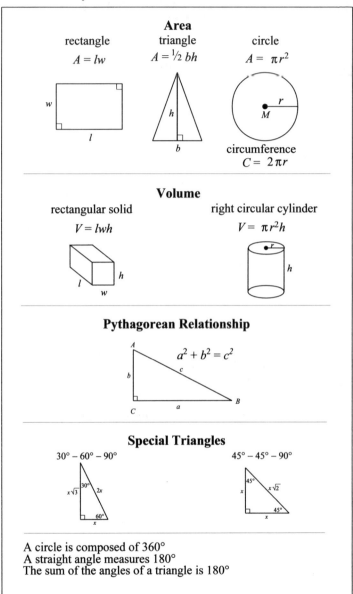

Area

rectangle

$A = lw$

triangle

$A = \frac{1}{2} bh$

circle

$A = \pi r^2$

w

l

h

b

r

M

circumference

$C = 2\pi r$

Volume

rectangular solid

$V = lwh$

right circular cylinder

$V = \pi r^2 h$

l *w* *h*

r *h*

Pythagorean Relationship

$a^2 + b^2 = c^2$

A

b

c

C

a

B

Special Triangles

$30° - 60° - 90°$

$x\sqrt{3}$ $30°$ $2x$

$60°$ x

$45° - 45° - 90°$

$45°$

x $x\sqrt{2}$

$45°$ x

A circle is composed of 360°
A straight angle measures 180°
The sum of the angles of a triangle is 180°

1. If each sack holds 9 pounds of brand X rice, how many sacks are needed to hold 20 kilograms of brand X rice?
   (1 kilogram = 2.25 pounds)
   (A) 1   (B) 5   (C) 9   (D) 20   (E) 45

2. If $y + 2$ is a positive integer, then y must be
   (A) even
   (B) odd
   (C) greater than -2
   (D) less than 2
   (E) positive

3. If $-5(7 + r - 4) = -30$, then $r =$
   (A) -3 (B) -9 (C) 0   (D) 2   (E) 3

4. If p is divided by 3, the remainder is 2.
   If p is divided by 4, the remainder is 1.
   If p is divided by 5, the remainder is 4.

   Which of the following could be the value of p?
   (A) 12   (B) 14   (C) 20   (D) 29   (E) 31

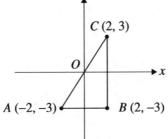

5. What is the area of $\triangle ABC$ in the figure above?
   (A) 3   (B) 6   (C) 12   (D) 18   (E) 24

6. A rectangular swimming pool is 50 feet long, 20 feet wide, and 6 feet deep. If water costs 30 cents per cubic foot, how much will it cost to fill the swimming pool completely?

   (A) $180
   (B) $200
   (C) $228
   (D) $1,800
   (E) $2,280

7. If the radius of a circle is multiplied by 3, its area increases by how many times?

   (A) 2   (B) 3   (C) 6   (D) 8   (E) 9

8. Sue is 5 years older than Roberta, and Tim is 6 years older than John. If Tim is 1 year older than Sue, which of the following must be true?

   I. Tim is 6 years older than Roberta.
   II. John and Roberta are the same age.
   III. Sue is 7 years older than John.

   (A) I only
   (B) II only
   (C) III only
   (D) I and II only
   (E) I, II, and III

9. In a basket, there are three electronic toys. One toy beeps every 8 minutes, another toy beeps every 10 minutes, and the third toy beeps every 12 minutes. All the toys beeped together at 1:00 a.m. When is the next time the three toys will beep together?

   (A) 1:12 a.m.
   (B) 1:30 a.m.
   (C) 3:00 a.m.
   (D) 3:12 a.m.
   (E) 5:00 p.m.

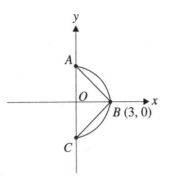

10. In the figure above, what is the perimeter of $\triangle ABC$ inscribed within the semicircle with center O?

(A) 9
(B) $6 + 3\sqrt{2}$
(C) $9 + 3\sqrt{3}$
(D) $6 + 6\sqrt{2}$
(E) $12\sqrt{2}$

11. If d is divisible by both 4 and 6, then which of the following must be true?

   I. d is divisible by 3.
  II. d is a multiple of 12.
 III. d is greater than 0.

(A) I only
(B) II only
(C) III only
(D) I and II only
(E) I, II, and III

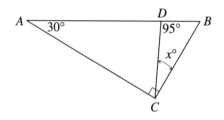

12. In $\triangle DBC$ above, $x =$
    (A) 15   (B) 25   (C) 35   (D) 45   (E) 55

13. If $p = x^n$, where n is a prime number, then p must be
    (A) a positive number
    (B) greater than 1
    (C) a prime number
    (D) an even number
    (E) a multiple of x

14. In a parking lot, there are 60 American, 20 Japanese, and E
    European cars. If 10% of all cars in the parking lot are
    Japanese, what is the value of E?
    (A) 20   (B) 40   (C) 60   (D) 120   (E) 200

15. If $A = \dfrac{p}{q}$, $B = \dfrac{q^2}{r}$, and $C = \dfrac{s}{r^2}$, what is $\dfrac{AB}{C}$?

    (A) $\dfrac{pqr}{s}$ (B) $\dfrac{pqs}{r^3}$ (C) $\dfrac{pr}{s}$ (D) $\dfrac{s}{pr}$ (E) $\dfrac{s}{pqr}$

16. A sheet of paper 8 units long and 6 units wide is rolled into a
    cylinder 8 units in height. What is the volume of the cylinder?

    (A) $\dfrac{9}{\pi}$ (B) $\dfrac{24}{\pi}$ (C) $\dfrac{48}{\pi}$ (D) $\dfrac{72}{\pi}$ (E) $\dfrac{96}{\pi}$

17. A set contains three numbers. The average (arithmetic mean) of the two smallest numbers in the set is 5 less than the average of all three numbers in the set. If the greatest number in the set is 5, what is the sum of the two smallest numbers in the set?

    (A) −20   (B) −10   (C) 5   (D) 10   (E) 20

18. A company's car-rental charges are $40 per day. If a customer rents a car for 4 or more consecutive days, the customer gets the last day free and pays only $30 per day for the other days. Ralph rents a car for 6 consecutive days, and Bill rents a car for 3 consecutive days. The average daily rate paid by Ralph is what percent of the average daily rate paid by Bill?

    (A) 62.5   (B) 65.5   (C) 75   (D) 80   (E) 133

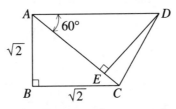

Note: Figure not drawn to scale.

19. In the figure above, if $AC = AD$, what is the area of $\triangle DEC$?

    (A) $\dfrac{\sqrt{2}}{2}$ (B) $\dfrac{\sqrt{3}}{2}$ (C) $\sqrt{2}$ (D) $\sqrt{3}$ (E) $2\sqrt{3}$

20. If $(x+4)(x+1) - (x-5)(x-2) = 0$, then $x^2 - x =$

    (A) $-\frac{1}{2}$ (B) $-\frac{1}{4}$ (C) 0   (D) $\frac{1}{2}$ (E) $\frac{1}{2}$

21. For any integer j, $j*$ is defined by

    $j* = j +$ the lowest prime number greater than j

    What is the value of $j*$ if $j = 5*$?

    (A) 5   (B) 7   (C) 12   (D) 13   (E) 25

22. The length and width of rectangular photographs developed by a lab are always in the ratio $(d-2):(d-5)$, respectively, where d is a constant. What is the width of a photograph developed by the lab if the area of the photograph is 40?
    (A) 3   (B) 5   (C) 8   (D) 10   (E) 11.5

23. Manuel traveled without stopping from Albertville to Bayville at an average speed of 40 miles per hour. On the return trip, he followed the same route without stopping at an average speed of 60 miles per hour. If Manuel spent a total of 20 hours on the entire two-way trip, what is the distance, in miles, between Albertville and Bayville?
    (A) 120   (B) 240   (C) 360   (D) 480   (E) 720

24. Three quarters of the value of Helena's estate x was divided equally among four charities. If each charity spent three quarters of the amount it received from the estate, which of the following represents the amount spent by each charity?
    (A) $\dfrac{3x}{64}$ (B) $\dfrac{9x}{64}$ (C) $\dfrac{3x}{16}$ (D) $\dfrac{9x}{16}$ (E) $\dfrac{3x}{4}$

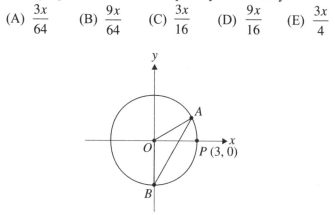

25. In the figure above, circle O has its center at the origin. If $\angle AOP = 30°$, what is the area of $\triangle OAB$?

     (A) $\sqrt{3}$ (B) $\dfrac{9\sqrt{3}}{4}$ (C) $3\sqrt{2}$ (D) $3\sqrt{3}$ (E) 9

STOP. IF YOU FINISH BEFORE TIME IS CALLED, CHECK YOUR WORK ON THIS SECTION ONLY. DO NOT WORK ON ANY OTHER SECTION IN THE TEST.

Time: 30 Minutes
31 Questions

In this section, choose the best answer for each question and blacken the corresponding space on the answer sheet.

Sentence Completion

DIRECTIONS

Each blank in the following sentences indicates that something has been omitted. Consider the lettered words beneath the sentence and choose the word or set of words that best fits the whole sentence.

1. Law enforcement officers and ---- of more than sixty citizens' groups are attempting to identify steps that can be taken to reduce crime in rural areas.
   (A) a bevy
   (B) a pack
   (C) a cohort
   (D) an amount
   (E) a coalition

2. Viewing nature as a potent and hostile force, the scientist describes the Alaskan landscape with words like ---- and ----.
   (A) mean . . base
   (B) cruel . . calm
   (C) stark . . hapless
   (D) ruthless . . brutal
   (E) tame . . awesome

3. Since television has taken tabloid journalism as its model, it is all but impossible to avoid a broadcast news program that ---- violent crime to the virtual ---- of all other kinds of news.

   (A) reports . . exclusion
   (B) disallows . . abandonment
   (C) encourages . . detriment
   (D) repudiates . . elimination
   (E) broadcasts . . admission

4. Dying sea birds along the Oregon coast may be ---- signs of potentially dangerous changes in the temperature of the ocean.

   (A) ominous
   (B) premature
   (C) invisible
   (D) literal
   (E) maritime

5. Ironically, the real ---- of the new lower taxes will be the ---- of the proposal who tried their hardest to defeat the bill.

   (A) profiteers . . opponents
   (B) antagonists . . advocates
   (C) beneficiaries . . adversaries
   (D) proprietors . . incumbents
   (E) freebooters . . dissenters

6. Normally a sympathetic and ---- judge of human character, in his autobiography Hall denounces many of his wisest friends as bumbling fools.

   (A) affectionate
   (B) forbearing
   (C) discerning
   (D) crotchety
   (E) parochial

7. Although the other politicians on the podium were ---- by the angry shouts from the audience, the mayor shrugged ---- and went on with his speech.

(A) enamored . . vindictively
(B) distraught . . irascibly
(C) amused . . cravenly
(D) inflamed . . heartily
(E) disturbed . . nonchalantly

8. A secret agency, like the CIA, that can conceal its secrets almost permanently, ---- operates outside the democratic process and is nearly impossible to consistently ----.

(A) presumably . . understand
(B) covertly . . decriminalize
(C) marginally . . penetrate
(D) occasionally . . predict
(E) regularly . . scrutinize

9. At the age of 34, Gould retired into ---- and ---- world, rarely leaving his Toronto hotel room and speaking to others only by letter or telephone.

(A) a convivial . . private
(B) a reclusive . . solitary
(C) a secluded . . gregarious
(D) a claustrophobic . . companionable
(E) an arcane . . arid

Analogies

DIRECTIONS

In each question below, you are given a related pair of words or phrases. Select the lettered pair that *best* expresses a relationship similar to that in the original pair.

10. BUTTERFLY : NET ::
    (A) aphid : insecticide
    (B) dust : dustpan
    (C) rabbit : snare
    (D) baseball : bat
    (E) bird : hunter

11. BASEBALLS : ORBS ::
    (A) dice : cubes
    (B) staircases : spirals
    (C) ice-creams : cones
    (D) circles : spheres
    (E) radii : circumferences

12. CALORIE : HEAT ::
    (A) exercise : weight
    (B) butter : fat
    (C) oven : cake
    (D) thermometer : centigrade
    (E) mile : distance

13. OIL : WATER ::
    (A) realism : fiction
    (B) milk : cream
    (C) tile : mosaic
    (D) boat : lake
    (E) syrup : tree

14. AMELIORATE : IMPROVEMENT ::
    (A) advertise : sale
    (B) expedite : punctuality
    (C) intercept : delivery
    (D) inoculate : immunity
    (E) extenuate : circumstance

15. FIRE : CONFLAGRATION ::
    (A) Armageddon : battle
    (B) hurricane : typhoon
    (C) flamboyance : ostentation
    (D) fear : terror
    (E) deluge : inundation

Critical Reading

DIRECTIONS

Questions follow each of the passages below. Using only the stated or implied information in each passage and in its introduction, if any, answer the questions.

Questions 16-22 are based on the following passage.

    While artists were winning new status in Renaissance society, there was an important shift in the attitudes toward the education of women that had prevailed in the fourteenth and fifteenth centuries. Early in the sixteenth century at the court of
(5) Federigo da Montefeltro in Urbino, Baldassare Castiglione wrote his *Il Cortegiano,* which was first published in 1528. Before the century was out, over thirty editions had been printed in Italy, France, England, and Spain. Castiglione devoted an entire chapter to the ideal feminine member of an
(10) aristocratic household such as Elisabetta Gonzaga, Duchess of Urbino, for whose entertainment and enlightenment the conversations in the book were supposedly held. Almost all

the attributes and accomplishments necessary to the male
courtier were also declared appropriate to the female, includ-
(15) ing a high level of educational attainment and the ability to
paint, play musical instruments and sing, write poetry, and
make witty, stimulating conversation. These ideas were not in
themselves new. They can be found much earlier in medieval
treatises on courtly behavior, but the invention of printing in
(20) the meantime meant that a far wider audience had access to
Castiglione's ideas of ideal courtly behavior than could ever
have learned about these customs in the Middle Ages. *Il
Cortegiano* was enormously popular; its influence on social
behavior and educational theory extended far beyond the
(25) Renaissance courts, where it originated, to all lesser noble
families and to all successful merchants wealthy enough to
emulate that way of life. Thus Castiglione helped to emanci-
pate women from the bondage of illiteracy and minimal education, extending the privileges and opportunities of a few
(30) women to those of a much wider social stratum. He made it
proper, even praiseworthy, for women to engage in a wide
range of artistic, musical, and literary pursuits, and if most
women only dabbled as amateurs and formal education for
women remained poor, there is still no shortage after the mid-
(35) sixteenth century of references to women who were regarded
by their contemporaries as exceptionally fine artists, musi-
cians, and writers.

Some proof of the influence Castiglione's ideas had on
the women who became painters can be found not only in
(40) their family origins but also and more significantly in the
ways they were presented to the world by themselves and
their biographers. Sofonisba Anguissola, the eldest daughter
of a provincial nobleman, fits neatly into the category of
daughters of minor aristocrats whose educational horizons
(45) were expanded by Castiglione. She and her sisters were all
taught to play musical instruments and to read Latin as well
as to paint. She signed her works with Latin inscriptions that

were always more elaborate than the simple "fecit" formula, and she twice painted herself playing a keyboard instrument.

(50) Thus she is a good example of the new female courtier, raised outside that closed society but well prepared, nevertheless, for her life at the court of Philip II in Madrid, where she became a lady-in-waiting to Queen Elizabeth of Valois.

16. According to the passage, Castiglione's *Il Cortegiano* was a
   (A) satire of the nobility
   (B) book defining ideal attributes of an aristocrat
   (C) tract advocating education for women
   (D) collection of conversations with noblewomen
   (E) treatise on art, music, and poetry

17. According to the passage, which of the following was most important in spreading Castiglione's ideas?
   (A) Their similarity to the ideas in medieval treatises
   (B) The influence of aristocratic women such as Elisabetta Gonzaga
   (C) The increasing influence of artists
   (D) The invention of printing
   (E) The growth of an aspiring merchant class

18. The passage implies all of the following EXCEPT:
   (A) Castiglione's book was popular beyond Italy.
   (B) In the Middle Ages, education for women wasn't considered important.
   (C) Castiglione favored a society not bound by a class structure.
   (D) Artists had a higher status in the Renaissance than they had in the Middle Ages.
   (E) A woman's education was inferior to a man's even in the latter part of the sixteenth century.

19. The word "emulate" in line 27 means
    (A) copy
    (B) refine
    (C) praise
    (D) disparage
    (E) define

20. The elaborate Latin inscriptions on Sofonisba Anguissola's paintings (lines 47-48) are mentioned in the passage as
    (A) a sign that some Renaissance women weren't afraid to go against convention
    (B) an example of the boastful behavior of the merchant class
    (C) an indication of the influence Castiglione's book had on women outside the court
    (D) an example of the intelligence of the ideal Renaissance woman
    (E) evidence of the importance of a thorough knowledge of Latin to artists who wanted to be successful

21. Which one of the following supports the author's point that Castiglione's influence extended beyond Renaissance courts?
    (A) After 1528, most women painters only dabbled as amateurs.
    (B) Elisabetta Gonzaga was amused and entertained by Castiglione's book.
    (C) Large numbers of women, at Castiglione's urging, demanded equality in the art world.
    (D) The quality of women's education improved dramatically after 1528.
    (E) Sofonisba Anguissola and her sisters were all taught to play musical instruments and read Latin.

22. The author's tone in this passage can best be described as
    (A) moralistic
    (B) objective
    (C) argumentative
    (D) somber
    (E) ironic

Questions 23-31 are based on the following passage.

In this passage, a paleoanthropologist speculates on the impact of environment on our human ancestors, based on fossils he found in the 1980s.

Our ancestors did not enter the plains like Oklahoma land-rushers racing to stake a claim in virgin territory; they were thrown into an environment already populated with highly successful savanna veterans. Like any species trying to carve
(5) a niche for itself in a new habitat, the hominids would have to sniff around the edges of the energy system, looking for food resources left unexploited by more established species. I doubt very much that *Homo* joined the ranks of the carnivores and took to hunting. Tools or no tools, how is a fruit 'n' nuts
(10) kind of generalist supposed to muscle a niche for itself between a five-hundred-pound lion and a pack of hyenas? The first hominids on the savanna did not have to compete with carnivores—they had only to stay out of their reach. Their real competitors would be other high-quality plant-food
(15) eaters, like the baboons, monkeys, and pigs. Like these other species, the hominids would have to come to terms with a fundamental fact of savanna habitat: Premium resources are rare and scattered. To keep alive, you will have to forage further, with greater reward attending whatever extra effort you
(20) put in.

But that's only half the problem. The savanna confounds the search for food in the dimension of *time* as well as space. People tend to think of savannas as dry, which is only partially

true. Some savannas receive as much as 100 inches of rain a
(25) year. What matters, however, is the timing of this rainfall. The
most distinguishing characteristic of the savanna environment is
seasonality. The rain comes in bursts. The periods in between
the dry seasons may last anywhere from two and a half to ten
months. The dry-season savanna is not just a thirsty version
(30) of the wet-season savanna. It is a different place altogether. In
the dry season the grass shrivels to a useless brown mat.
Where there was food, there is dust. In low elevations the heat
is intense, and even on the relatively cool plateaus like the
Serengeti, there is little shade to escape to from the sun. The
(35) herbivores, dispersed during the wet season, either migrate
away or flock to permanent sources of water. There many die
of starvation, or fall victim to the predators who await their
coming. Animals adapted to higher-quality plant foods suffer
just as much. They stand in double jeopardy: As each parcel
(40) of their range grows increasingly impoverished, the drying up
of waterholes keeps them bound to a smaller and smaller for-
aging area.

To every animal on the savanna, the dry season represents a chasm of lean times that has to be bridged year after
(45) year. The first thing an animal does when faced with a lapse
in resources is cut down on activity to save energy. Not many
mammals have evolved the radical extreme of hibernation,
but most show a falling off of play, socializing, and repro-
ducing during the hard months. But rarely is energy saving
(50) alone enough to allow survival until the rains return. Each
animal has to make a crucial decision: either to start eating
lower-quality foods like mature leaves, seeds, and stems that
are still abundant in the dry season, or to find ways to win
access to higher-quality foods previously out of reach.

(55)   I think it was this dry-season "decision" that really forced
the branching in the hominid line. In response to the season-
al stress, some populations of *afarensis* developed the cus-
tomized chewing equipment—those massive jaws and heliport

(60) molars—that would enable the robust australopithecines* to cope with the tough, low-quality vegetation available in the dry season. But another population took a second route. Building on their history as resourceful, omnivorous primates, the ancestors of *Homo* began to poke around in the dry season looking for new opportunities to get at out-of-reach

(65) foods with high payoffs. They did not use specialized jaws and teeth to get at these prized goods. They used their heads.

*Name given to a prehuman species; the author believes that some members of a species called *Australopithecus afarensis* became the ancestors of the human species (*Homo*) whereas others did not.

23. According to the passage, humans' ancestors had to compete hard for food because they were
   (A) physically and mentally weaker than the other inhabitants of the savanna
   (B) carnivorous (meat-eating) creatures in an area with limited resources
   (C) newcomers to a habitat populated with established species
   (D) unable to match the hunting skills of other carnivores and unwilling to eat low-quality foods
   (E) the natural prey of most of the other species on the savanna

24. The word "hominids" in line 5 refers to
   (A) humans' ancestors
   (B) generalists
   (C) low-quality plant eaters
   (D) human beings
   (E) carnivores

25. The phrase "fruit 'n' nuts kind of generalist" (lines 9 10) most likely refers to the fact that hominids
    (A) ate both meat and plants
    (B) were smarter than other species
    (C) were similar to predators such as hyenas
    (D) lacked aggressive tendencies
    (E) ate a variety of high-quality plant foods

26. According to the passage, which of the following was the most significant problem for plant-eaters on the savanna?
    (A) Predators
    (B) Rainfall up to 100 inches a year
    (C) Long dry periods
    (D) Limited shade and heavy dust
    (E) Scarcity of water holes

27. According to the passage, during dry periods on the savanna all of the following are likely to occur EXCEPT
    (A) increased reproductive activity
    (B) migration of plant-eating animals
    (C) reduction of animal foraging areas
    (D) greater danger from predators
    (E) decreased socialization

28. The author describes the conditions on the savanna primarily
    (A) to illustrate the difficulties facing both plant-eating and meat-eating species
    (B) to explain the split between carnivores and herbivores
    (C) to set up a theory about the branching of the hominid line
    (D) as a contrast to the situation facing Oklahoma land-rushers
    (E) to create a vivid picture of the prehistoric world that produced humans' ancestors

29. Lions and hyenas are linked in line 11 because
    (A) they both travel in groups
    (B) one is a carnivore and one a herbivore (plant-eater)
    (C) they are both physically imposing but mentally weak
    (D) they are both carnivores
    (E) they were both cleverer than early hominids

30. If true, which of the following statements would contradict the author's theory?
    (A) Less plant life than previously believed existed on the savanna.
    (B) More carnivorous than herbivorous species existed on the savanna.
    (C) The jaws of fossils found on the savanna vary considerably in size.
    (D) Temperatures on the savanna were an average of 20 degrees lower than previously believed.
    (E) Rain fell heavily throughout the year on the prehistoric savanna.

31. The last sentence of the passage
    (A) proves the author's theory about humans' ancestors
    (B) makes an ironic point about the origin of the human species
    (C) suggests that the search for food was related to the development of the brain
    (D) implies that had it not been for the development of tools, early humans wouldn't have survived
    (E) suggests that early humans outwitted their predators.

STOP. IF YOU FINISH BEFORE TIME IS CALLED, CHECK YOUR WORK ON THIS SECTION ONLY. DO NOT WORK ON ANY OTHER SECTION IN THE TEST.

Time: 30 Minutes
25 Questions

DIRECTIONS

This section is composed of two types of questions. Use the 30 minutes allotted to answer both question types. Your scratch work should be done on any available space in the section.

Notes

(1) All numbers used are real numbers.
(2) Calculators may be used.
(3) Some problems may be accompanied by figures or diagrams. These figures are drawn as accurately as possible EXCEPT when it is stated in a specific problem that a figure is not drawn to scale. The figures and diagrams are meant to provide information useful in solving the problem or problems. Unless otherwise stated, all figures and diagrams lie in a plane.

Data That May Be Used for Reference

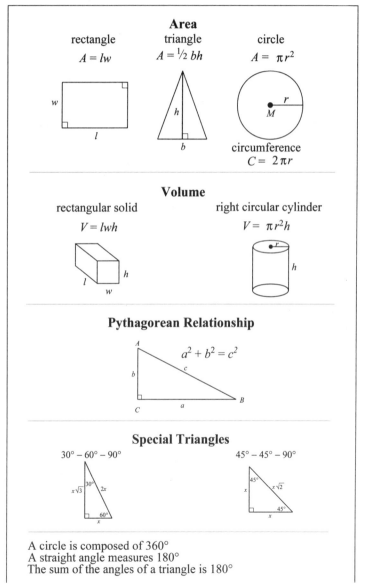

Area

rectangle

$A = lw$

triangle

$A = \frac{1}{2}bh$

circle

$A = \pi r^2$

circumference

$C = 2\pi r$

Volume

rectangular solid

$V = lwh$

right circular cylinder

$V = \pi r^2 h$

Pythagorean Relationship

$a^2 + b^2 = c^2$

Special Triangles

$30° - 60° - 90°$

$45° - 45° - 90°$

A circle is composed of 360°
A straight angle measures 180°
The sum of the angles of a triangle is 180°

Quantitative Comparison

DIRECTIONS

In this section, you will be given two quantities, one in column A and one in column B. You are to determine a relationship between the two quantities and mark—

(A) if the quantity in column A is greater than the quantity in column B
(B) if the quantity in column B is greater than the quantity in column A
(C) if the quantities are equal
(D) if the comparison cannot be determined from the information that is given

AN (E) RESPONSE WILL NOT BE SCORED.

Notes

(1) Sometimes, information concerning one or both of the quantities to be compared is given. This information is not boxed and is centered above the two columns.
(2) All numbers used are real numbers. Letters such as *a, b, m,* and *x* represent real numbers.
(3) In a given question, if the same symbol is used in column A and column B, that symbol stands for the same value in each column.

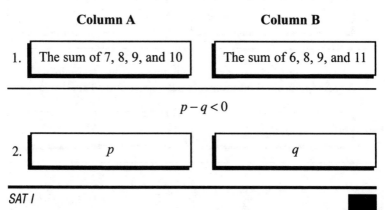

Column A	Column B
1. The sum of 7, 8, 9, and 10	The sum of 6, 8, 9, and 11

$$p - q < 0$$

| 2. p | q |

Column A   **Column B**

Think of a number. Double it. Add another number x to your answer. Divide this sum by 2.

Subtract from this quotient the number you initially thought of.

3. | The number you are left with | Half of x |

4. | Twice the area of a right triangle of sides 3", 4", and 5" | The area of a right triangle of sides 6", 8", and 10" |

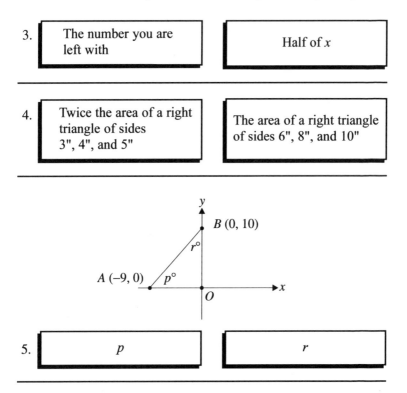

5. | p | r |

A = sum of all even integers between 2 and 10 inclusive.
B = sum of all odd integers between 1 and 11 inclusive.

6. | $B - A$ | 5 |

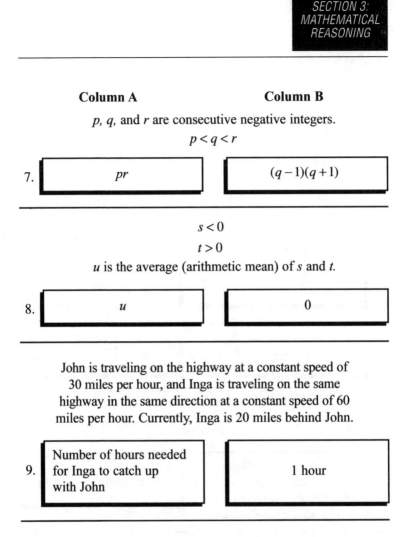

Column A   **Column B**

p, q, and r are consecutive negative integers.

$$p < q < r$$

7. pr $(q-1)(q+1)$

$$s < 0$$
$$t > 0$$

u is the average (arithmetic mean) of s and t.

8. u 0

John is traveling on the highway at a constant speed of
30 miles per hour, and Inga is traveling on the same
highway in the same direction at a constant speed of 60
miles per hour. Currently, Inga is 20 miles behind John.

9. Number of hours needed
    for Inga to catch up
    with John   1 hour

Column A   Column B

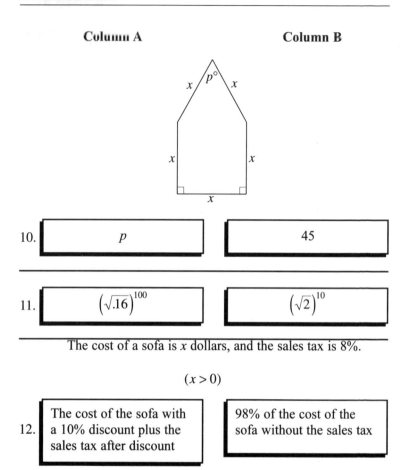

10. | p | 45

11. | $\left(\sqrt{.16}\right)^{100}$ | $\left(\sqrt{2}\right)^{10}$

The cost of a sofa is x dollars, and the sales tax is 8%.

$(x > 0)$

12. | The cost of the sofa with a 10% discount plus the sales tax after discount | 98% of the cost of the sofa without the sales tax

Column A   **Column B**

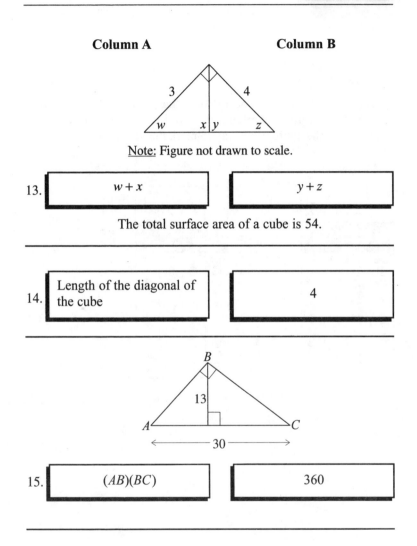

Note: Figure not drawn to scale.

13. | $w + x$ | | $y + z$ |

The total surface area of a cube is 54.

14. | Length of the diagonal of the cube | | 4 |

15. | $(AB)(BC)$ | | 360 |

Grid-In Questions

DIRECTIONS

Questions 16-25 require you to solve the problem and enter your answer by carefully marking the circles on the special grid. Examples of the appropriate way to mark the grid follow.

Answer: 3.7   **Answer: 1/2**

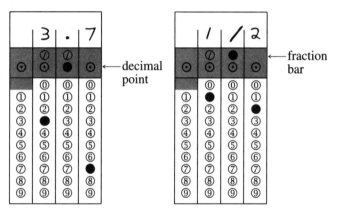

←decimal point   ←fraction bar

Answer: $1\frac{1}{2}$

Do not grid in mixed numbers in the form of mixed numbers.
Always change mixed numbers to improper fractions or decimals.

Change to 1.5   or   Change to 3/2

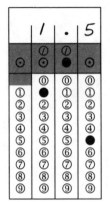 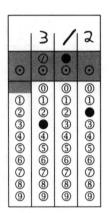

Answer: 123

Space permitting, answers may start in any column. Each grid-in
answer below is correct.

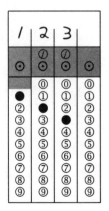

Note: Circles must be filled in correctly to receive credit. Mark only one circle in each column. No credit will be given if more than one circle in a column is marked. Example:

Answer: 258

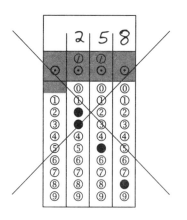

No credit!!!!

Answer: 8/9

Accuracy of decimals: Always enter the most accurate decimal value that the grid will accommodate. For example: An answer such as .8888 . . . can be gridded as .888 or .889. Gridding this value as .8, .88, or .89 is considered inaccurate and therefore **not acceptable.** The acceptable grid-ins of 8/9 are

8/9   .888   .889

Be sure to write your answers in the boxes at the top of the circles before doing your gridding. Although writing out the answers above the columns is not required, it is very important to ensure accuracy. Even though some problems may have more than one correct answer, grid only **one answer.** Grid-in questions contain no negative answers.

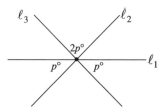

16. In the figure above, ℓ_1, ℓ_2, and ℓ_3 are straight lines intersecting at the same point. What is the value of p?

17. If the perimeter of a square of length $(q-5)$ is 100, what is the value of q?

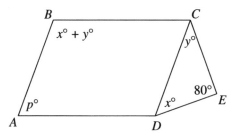

Tick marks on the line above are equally spaced.

18. If the leftmost tick mark shown above has a value of zero, what is the value of T?

19. In the figure above, $ABCD$ is a parallelogram. What is the value of p?

20. A company's second-year earnings were 10% more than its first-year earnings. The company's third-year earnings were 10% less than its second-year earnings. The company's third-year earnings were what percent of its first-year earnings?

21. A password has three slots. The first slot has to contain a letter of the alphabet, and each of the other two slots has to contain a number from 0 to 9 (inclusive). The same numeric digit cannot occur twice. How many different passwords are possible? (Assume that an upper-case letter of the alphabet is the same as its lower-case counterpart.)

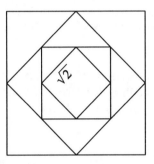

22. The smallest of the four squares shown in the figure above has side of length $\sqrt{2}$. The smaller squares are formed by connecting the midpoints of the larger squares. What is the area of the largest square?

23. For any integer k, let $k*$ be defined by

$$k* = k + 8, \text{if } k \leq 8$$
$$k* = k - 8, \text{if } k > 8$$

What is the value of $(7* + 9*)*$?

24. A set contains five different positive integers, 7, 8, t, 6, and u. The total of the integers in the set is 30, and the median is 6. What is the value of t if u is greater than t?

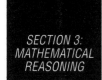

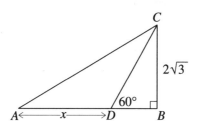

25. In the figure above, the area of $\triangle ABC = 6\sqrt{3}$. What is the value of *x*?

STOP. IF YOU FINISH BEFORE TIME IS CALLED, CHECK YOUR WORK ON THIS SECTION ONLY. DO NOT WORK ON ANY OTHER SECTION IN THE TEST.

Time: 30 Minutes
35 Questions

In this section, choose the best answer for each question and blacken the corresponding space on the answer sheet.

Sentence Completion

DIRECTIONS

Each blank in the following sentences indicates that something has been omitted. Consider the lettered words beneath the sentence and choose the word or set of words that best fits the whole sentence.

1. The lobby was ---- enough to allow a number of armchairs to be spread about with no sense of crowding.
   (A) handsome
   (B) munificent
   (C) spacious
   (D) baroque
   (E) constricted

2. Predictably, the students who were ---- in mathematics often ---- in physics.
   (A) competent . . prevailed
   (B) adept . . excelled
   (C) deficient . . compensated
   (D) practiced . . stumbled
   (E) inadequate . . prospered

3. Early in the twentieth century, urban Americans began to seek wilderness areas as ---- to the stress of civilization.
   (A) an antagonist
   (B) a façade
   (C) an antidote
   (D) a collaborator
   (E) an extension

4. The fear of ---- of the currencies of Switzerland and Germany has ---- a widespread selling of both the Swiss franc and the German mark.
   (A) a devaluation . . effected
   (B) a deterioration . . inhibited
   (C) a shortage . . precipitated
   (D) an appreciation . . encouraged
   (E) a stability . . realigned

5. The Conservative party's failure to win a single seat in Scotland or Wales turned the election that might have been only a heavy defeat into a ----.
   (A) paradox
   (B) conjecture
   (C) rebuff
   (D) debacle
   (E) discomfiture

6. Compared to the efficient and streamlined broadcasts of today, the ---- television programs of the 1940s have ---- appearance, as if they happened spontaneously.
   (A) sophisticated . . an amateurish
   (B) live . . a refined
   (C) antique . . a smooth
   (D) methodical . . a haphazard
   (E) rudimentary . . an improvisational

7. Archeologists attribute the remarkable ---- of the gunboat to the cold, dark, airless waters at the site where it was discovered.
   (A) restoration
   (B) preservation
   (C) delineation
   (D) deportation
   (E) renovation

8. Before eventually accepting George Orwell's famous satiric fable *Animal Farm,* the publisher ---- turned it down with the ---- comment, "They do well in England, but it's impossible to sell animal stories in the United States."
   (A) definitively . . terse
   (B) ultimately . . perceptive
   (C) tentatively . . insightful
   (D) initially . . commercial
   (E) originally . . verbose

9. Whether they express ---- or ----, there is no shortage of divergent strong opinions about the inspector general, who is responsible for policing the police department.
   (A) animosity . . rancor
   (B) praise . . vilification
   (C) acceptance . . indifference
   (D) approbation . . support
   (E) condemnation . . detraction

10. Many church leaders in South Africa are vigilant and eloquent ---- of respect for the ---- dignity of every human being.
    (A) spokespeople . . instinctive
    (B) prognosticators . . essential
    (C) emissaries . . irrepressible
    (D) preachers . . irreconcilable
    (E) advocates . . innate

Analogies

DIRECTIONS

In each question below, you are given a related pair of words or phrases. Select the lettered pair that *best* expresses a relationship similar to that in the original pair.

11. TABLESPOON : CUP ::
    (A) fork : plate
    (B) ounce : pint
    (C) hammer : nail
    (D) stove : oven
    (E) radius : circle

12. CAFFEINE : SLEEP ::
    (A) exorcist : muscle
    (B) censorship : television
    (C) leg : foot
    (D) catalyst : reaction
    (E) smog : respiration

13. WORDS : LYRIC ::
    (A) costumes : play
    (B) notes : song
    (C) paintings : museum
    (D) mosaic : tile
    (E) plot : novel

14. COMEDY : THEATER ::
    (A) skater : rink
    (B) film : festival
    (C) laughter : joke
    (D) tiger : jungle
    (E) game : stadium

15. BROKER : BROKERAGE ::
    (A) thermometer : mercury
    (B) florist : flower
    (C) astronomer : observatory
    (D) tire : automobile
    (E) shoemaker : cobbler

16. LAUGH : GUFFAW ::
    (A) sip : drink
    (B) prowl : trudge
    (C) hasten : run
    (D) eat : gobble
    (E) walk : saunter

17. LEVEE : FLOOD ::
    (A) dam : river
    (B) vaccine : polio
    (C) lighthouse : storm
    (D) cavity : dentist
    (E) landing : steamboat

18. DESPAIRING : HOPE ::
    (A) indigent : money
    (B) inauspicious : sincerity
    (C) angry : control
    (D) gluttonous : manners
    (E) patient : suffering

19. ALARM : WARN ::
    (A) ambulance : speed
    (B) yeast : leaven
    (C) table : dine
    (D) shoe : walk
    (E) door : open

20. MAGMA . ROCK ..
    (A) water : ice
    (B) forest : wood
    (C) geyser : heat
    (D) volcano : lava
    (E) plant : sunlight

21. PALINDROME : RADAR ::
    (A) airport : tower
    (B) metaphor : simile
    (C) onomatopoeia : buzz
    (D) submarine : sonar
    (E) meter : poetry

22. INVETERATE : SUPERFICIAL ::
    (A) frugal : chary
    (B) profound : compliant
    (C) arduous : ephemeral
    (D) peremptory : imperious
    (E) conspicuous : imperceptible

23. ARCHAIC : ANTIQUATED ::
    (A) difficult : impossible
    (B) aerobic : anaerobic
    (C) prodigal : wasteful
    (D) unequal : equated
    (E) prehistoric : modern

Critical Reading

DIRECTIONS

Questions follow each of the passages below. Using only the stated or implied information in the passage and in its introduction, if any, answer the questions.

Questions 24-35 are based on the following passage.

The crisis between the British colonies and the mother country was, in essence, a quarrel over the nature of authority. The form in which that conflict presented itself was a contention over that most basic "right," the right to the control of one's
(5) own property. As the colonists were disposed to put it, no one had authority to take money out of their pockets without their consent. While Parliament had, as we have seen, fiercely resisted the right of the king to take money out of *Parliament's* pockets, or, more accurately, out of the pockets of the class of
(10) persons represented by the members of Parliament, they had no particular scruples about taking money out of the pockets of their American cousins, or subjects. In fact, the objections of the Americans, far from appearing to Parliament and its ministers to be a proper concern for the rights of Englishmen
(15) not to be taxed without representation, seemed captious and indeed little short of treasonable. British constitutional theorists insisted the colonists were "virtually" represented in Parliament, a word that nowhere appeared in the American political lexicon and the colonists suspected had been invent-
(20) ed for the occasion. The argument that large numbers of Englishmen in cities like Birmingham and Manchester sent no representatives to Parliament and yet were obliged to pay taxes levied by that body failed to impress the Americans. They could not understand how two wrongs might make a
(25) right.

The American colonists, long accustomed to managing
their own affairs to a degree quite unprecedented in the history
of any other colonies, had no intention of giving ground. From
their perspective across three thousand miles of ocean it seemed
(30) that Parliament was disposed to act frequently in an arbitrary
manner and to do so with an ineffable self-righteousness.
From the time of the passage of the Stamp Act in 1765, armed
conflict between the colonies and the mother country was
probably inevitable. In the view of the colonists the British
(35) government was acting in an unconstitutional manner and they
had substantial support in that opinion from such English
Whig leaders as William Pitt and Edmund Burke. The
Americans cited Magna Charta, the Petition of Right from the
era of the English Civil War, and the Proclamation of Rights
(40) that accompanied the Glorious Revolution and the ascent to
the throne of William and Mary. They also cited the British
constitution, which proved a demanding task, since the constitution, being unwritten, was subject to an even wider range
of interpretation than the later written constitutions, which,
(45) almost without exception, derived from it. After having fished
in these murky waters for several years with uncertain results,
the colonial political theorists began, with obvious reluctance,
to shift their ground from arguments based on the British constitution to arguments based on the God-given immutable
(50) rights of man, of which the British constitution was only one
manifestation.
Even before the Stamp Act in 1765, the passage the year
before of the so-called Revenue Act, designed to raise revenue
for the British treasury and tighten up the laws regulating colo-
(55) nial trade, had, in the words of James Otis, a Massachusetts
politician and leader in the resistance to parliamentary taxation, "set people a-thinking, in six months more than they had
in their lives before." James Otis wrote a tract entitled "The
Rights of the British Colonies Asserted and Proved," in which
(60) he spelled out the essence of the colonial position in a way

that was hardly improved on in the years prior to the Revolution. Otis began his essay with an account of the nature of authority, quoting "the incomparable" James Harrington's *Oceana*. Power was allied with property. The

(65) wealthy man had power although he might not have "much more wit than a mole or musquash." But it did not follow from this "that government is rightfully founded on property, alone." Nor is it "founded on grace. . . . Nor on force. . . . Nor on compact? Nor property?" Not altogether on any or all of

(70) these. Has it then, Otis asked his readers, "any solid foundation? and chief corner stone, but what accident, chance or confusion may lay one moment and destroy the next?"

In Otis's view it had "an everlasting foundation in the unchangeable will of God, the author of nature, whose laws

(75) never vary. The same omniscient, omnipotent, infinitely good and gracious Creator of the Universe, who has been pleased to make it necessary that what we call matter should gravitate, for the celestial bodies to roll round their axes, dance their orbits and perform their various revolutions in that beautiful

(80) order and concert, which we all admire, has made it equally necessary that . . . the different sexes should sweetly attract each other, form societies of single families of which larger bodies and communities are as naturally, mechanically and necessarily combined, as the dew of Heaven and the soft dis-

(85) tilling rain is collected by all the enliv'ning heat of the sun." Government was thus founded "on the necessities of our nature. It is by no means an arbitrary thing, depending merely on compact or human will for its existence."

24. According to the passage, pro-British political theorists argued that the colonists
   (A) already had too much freedom
   (B) were in effect represented in Parliament
   (C) had no rights to property under the British constitution
   (D) were three thousand miles away from England and therefore didn't understand the mother country's needs
   (E) did not present a clear argument for their point of view

25. The most likely reason that the citizens of Manchester and Birmingham didn't react as the colonists did to taxation without representation is that
   (A) the colonies were far away and accustomed to largely managing their own affairs, whereas Manchester and Birmingham were cities within England
   (B) the citizens of Manchester and Birmingham received many more benefits from taxation than the colonists and weren't interested in governmental structure
   (C) the citizens of Manchester and Birmingham weren't as courageous and intelligent as the colonists
   (D) unlike the colonists, the citizens of Manchester and Birmingham understood the British constitution
   (E) Manchester and Birmingham, unlike the colonies, were viewed favorably by Parliament and therefore had nothing to fear from a lack of representation

26. In the context of the passage, "their consent" in lines 6-7 can be seen as another way of saying
   (A) freedom
   (B) consideration
   (C) taxation
   (D) representation
   (E) basic rights

27. The implication of the phrase "or, more accurately, out of the pockets of the class of persons represented by the members of Parliament" (lines 9-10) is that

   (A) members of Parliament were opposed to equality
   (B) England's poorest citizens were not represented in Parliament
   (C) Parliament saw its function as opposing the king's absolute authority
   (D) the members of Parliament were unscrupulous and received many bribes
   (E) Parliament believed in taxing only the poorest citizens

28. Based on information in the passage, the Stamp Act of 1765 probably

   (A) restricted the colonists' use of the British mail system
   (B) limited the colonists' freedom of speech
   (C) was a form of taxing the colonists
   (D) was a form of punishing the colonists for treasonable behavior
   (E) was dictated by the English monarchy

29. According to the passage, which of the following would NOT support the principles behind the colonists' position on taxation without representation?

   (A) the Magna Charta
   (B) the British constitution
   (C) the writings of Edmund Burke
   (D) the Revenue Act
   (E) the Petition of Right

30. Which of the following caused the colonial political theorists to "shift their ground" (line 48) in their arguments?
    (A) The "ineffable self-righteousness" of the British Parliament and its increasing hostility to the colonists
    (B) The tracts of James Otis
    (C) The fact that the British constitution was unwritten and subject to changing interpretations
    (D) The examples of Manchester and Birmingham cited by the British Parliament in its arguments against the colonists
    (E) The escalating measures to tax the colonists and restrain their freedom to engage in trade

31. According to James Otis's tract "The Rights of the British Colonies Asserted and Proved," property
    (A) was sacred
    (B) was the basis of government
    (C) should be divided equally among members of a community
    (D) was linked to power
    (E) formed the "everlasting foundation" of constitutions

32. Based on the quotation from "The Rights of the British Colonies Asserted and Proved," which of the following statements clearly expresses Otis's point?
    (A) Government that governs least governs best.
    (B) Power corrupts, and absolute power corrupts absolutely.
    (C) Human rights come from God, not from man.
    (D) Government is based on a compact between men of good faith.
    (E) Without law, the world is no better than a jungle.

33. The best meaning for "mechanically" in line 83 is
    (A) automatically
    (B) without design
    (C) in a complex manner
    (D) artificially
    (E) efficiently

34. Otis uses the examples of celestial bodies following their orbits and the sweet attraction between the sexes to emphasize
    (A) different views of government
    (B) that one needs to recognize one's proper station in life
    (C) that all natural and human law has the same origin
    (D) that Church is superior to State
    (E) the beauty, variety, and unpredictability of the universe

35. The main purpose of this passage is to
    (A) examine the role of political theorists in the American Revolution
    (B) describe the cruelty of the British Parliament and the "treasonable acts" of the colonists
    (C) show how Parliament and the colonists disagreed about the nature of authority and the origin of human rights
    (D) show the role of the British constitution in the colonists' quarrel with Parliament
    (E) trace the history of Parliament's imposition of taxes on the colonies

STOP. IF YOU FINISH BEFORE TIME IS CALLED, CHECK YOUR WORK ON THIS SECTION ONLY. DO NOT WORK ON ANY OTHER SECTION IN THE TEST.

Time: 15 Minutes
10 Questions

DIRECTIONS

Solve each problem in this section by using the information given and your own mathematical calculations, insights, and problem-solving skills. Then select the one correct answer of the five choices given and mark the corresponding circle on your answer sheet. Use the available space on the page for your scratch work.

Notes

(1) All numbers used are real numbers.
(2) Calculators may be used.
(3) Some problems may be accompanied by figures or diagrams. These figures are drawn as accurately as possible EXCEPT when it is stated in a specific problem that a figure is not drawn to scale. The figures and diagrams are meant to provide information useful in solving the problem or problems. Unless otherwise stated, all figures and diagrams lie in a plane.

Data That May Be Used for Reference

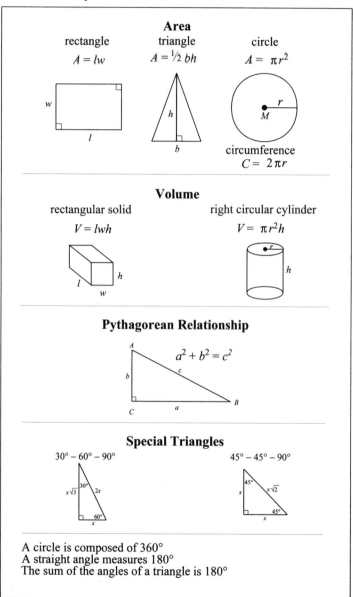

Area

rectangle

$A = lw$

triangle

$A = \frac{1}{2} bh$

circle

$A = \pi r^2$

circumference

$C = 2\pi r$

Volume

rectangular solid

$V = lwh$

right circular cylinder

$V = \pi r^2 h$

Pythagorean Relationship

$a^2 + b^2 = c^2$

Special Triangles

$30° - 60° - 90°$

$45° - 45° - 90°$

A circle is composed of 360°
A straight angle measures 180°
The sum of the angles of a triangle is 180°

1. If $\dfrac{5}{a+b} = 25$, what is the value of $a + b$?

(A) -20 (B) $\frac{1}{5}$ (C) 1 (D) 5 (E) 20

2. If $k + m = n + p$, and $m = n + 1$, what is the value of k in terms of p?

(A) $1 - p$
(B) $p - 1$
(C) $p + 1$
(D) $2n - 1 + p$
(E) $2n + 1 + p$

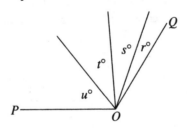

3. In the figure above, $\angle POQ$ is $120°$, and

$$s = 2r$$
$$t = 3r$$
$$u = 4r$$

What is the value of t?

(A) 12 (B) 24 (C) 36 (D) 48 (E) 60

4. From her home, Brigitte drove 60 miles due east to Addison, and from Addison, she drove 80 miles due north to Belville. If from Belville she takes a highway that heads directly to her home, how many <u>fewer</u> miles did she drive directly from Belville to her home, compared to her drive to Belville through Addison?

(A) 20 (B) 40 (C) 60 (D) 80 (E) 100

Questions 5-6 refer to the following table.

Grizzly Bears Seen in Denali National Park

Year	Number
1970	320
1975	400
1980	450
1985	450
1990	360
1995	400

5. According to the table, in which of the following periods was there the greatest increase in the number of grizzly bears seen?
(A) 1970–1975
(B) 1975–1980
(C) 1980–1985
(D) 1985–1990
(E) 1990–1995

6. The number of grizzly bears seen in 1995 is what percent of the number seen in 1970?
(A) 25   (B) 80   (C) 120   (D) 125   (E) 140

7. If $2p + 4$ is divisible by 9, then which of the following CAN-NOT be a value of p?
(A) −11   (B) 2.5   (C) 7   (D) 9   (E) 16

8. A line 3 units long is drawn from the origin of an xy-coordinate plane. Which of the following could be the coordinates of a point on the line if the slope of the line is 1?
(A) (3, 1)
(B) (−3, 1)
(C) (−1, −1)
(D) (1, 3)
(E) (−1, 3)

9. If $p + 3q + 4r - 5s = 10$ and $3p + 9q = 12$, what is the value of $8r - 10s$?

   (A)   4
   (B)   6
   (C) 12
   (D) 28
   (E) It cannot be determined from the information given.

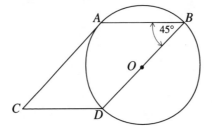

10. In the figure above, if the radius of the circle with center at O is 5 and points A, B, and D are on the circle, what is the area of parallelogram $ABDC$?

   (A) 25   (B) $25\sqrt{2}$ (C) $25\sqrt{3}$ (D) 50   (E) $50\sqrt{2}$

STOP. IF YOU FINISH BEFORE TIME IS CALLED, CHECK YOUR WORK ON THIS SECTION ONLY. DO NOT WORK ON ANY OTHER SECTION IN THE TEST.

Time: 15 Minutes
15 Questions

In this section, choose the best answer for each question and blacken the corresponding space on the answer sheet.

Critical Reading

<small>DIRECTIONS</small>

Questions follow the two passages below. Using only the stated or implied information in each passage and in its introduction, if any, answer the questions.

Questions 1-15 are based on the following passages.

The first passage below is from the 1892 autobiography of Frederick Douglass, a runaway slave who became an adviser to Abraham Lincoln and a United States diplomat. The second passage is from a book of essays by the African-American writer and scholar W.E.B. Du Bois; it was originally published in 1903.

Passage 1

On an antislavery tour through the West, in company with H. Ford Douglas, a young colored man of fine intellect and much promise, and my old friend John Jones (both now deceased), we stopped at a hotel in Janesville, and were seated by our-
(5)   selves to take our meals where all the barroom loafers of the town could stare at us. Thus seated, I took occasion to say loud enough for the crowd to hear me, that I had just been out to the stable, and had made a great discovery. Asked by Mr. Jones what my discovery was, I said that I saw there black

(10) horses and white horses eating together in peace from the same trough, from which I inferred that the horses of Janesville were more civilized than its people. The crowd saw the hit, and broke out into a good-natured laugh. We were afterward entertained at the same table with other guests.

(15) Many years ago, on my way from Cleveland to Buffalo on one of the lake steamers, the gong sounded for supper. There was a rough element on board, such as at that time might be found anywhere between Buffalo and Chicago. It was not to be trifled with, especially when hungry. At the first

(20) sound of the gong there was a furious rush for the table. From prudence, more than from lack of appetite, I waited for the second table, as did several others. At this second table I took a seat far apart from the few gentlemen scattered along its side, but directly opposite a well-dressed, fine-featured man

(25) of the fairest complexion, high forehead, golden hair, and light beard. His whole appearance told me he was *somebody*. I had been seated but a minute or two when the steward came to me and roughly ordered me away. I paid no attention to him, but proceeded to take my supper, determined not to

(30) leave unless compelled to do so by superior force, and, being young and strong, I was not entirely unwilling to risk the consequences of such a contest. A few moments passed, when on each side of my chair there appeared a stalwart of my own race. I glanced at the gentleman opposite. His brow was knit,

(35) his color changed from white to scarlet and his eyes were full of fire. I saw the lightning flash, but I could not tell where it would strike. Before my sable brethren could execute their captain's order, and just about as they were to lay violent hands upon me, a voice from that man of golden hair and fiery

(40) eyes resounded like a clap of summer thunder. "Let the gentleman alone! I am not ashamed to take my tea with Mr. Douglass." His was a voice to be obeyed, and my right to my seat and my supper was no more disputed.

Passage 2

Between me and the other world there is ever an unasked
(45) question: unasked by some through feelings of delicacy; by
others through the difficulty of rightly framing it. All, nevertheless, flutter round it. They approach me in a half-hesitant
sort of way, eye me curiously or compassionately, and then
instead of saying directly, How does it feel to be a problem?
(50) they say, I know an excellent colored man in my town; or, I
fought at Mechanicsville*; or, Do not these Southern outrages
make your blood boil? At these I smile, or am interested, or
reduce the boiling to a simmer, as the occasion may require.
To the real question, How does it feel to be a problem? I
(55) answer seldom a word.

And yet, being a problem is a strange experience,—peculiar
even for one who has never been anything else, save perhaps
in babyhood and in Europe. It is in the early days of rollick-
ing boyhood that the revelation first burst upon me, all in a
(60) day, as it were. I remember well when the shadow swept
across me. In a wee wooden schoolhouse, something put it
into the boys' and girls' heads to buy gorgeous visiting-
cards—ten cents a package—and exchange. The exchange
was merry, till one girl, a tall newcomer, refused my card,—
(65) refused it peremptorily, with a glance. Then it dawned on me
with a certain suddenness that I was different from the others;
or like, mayhap, in heart and life and longing, but shut out
from their world by a vast veil. I had thereafter no desire to
tear down that veil, to creep through; I held all beyond it in
(70) common contempt, and lived above it in a region of blue sky
and great wandering shadows. The sky was bluest when I
could beat my mates at examination-time, or beat them at a
foot-race, or even beat their stringy heads. Alas, with the
years all this fine contempt began to fade; for the worlds I
(75) longed for, and all their dazzling opportunities, were theirs,

*An 1862 Civil War battle in Virginia

not mine. But they should not keep these prizes, I said; some, all, I would wrest from them. Just how I would do it I could never decide: by reading law, by healing the sick, by telling the wonderful tales that swam in my head,—some way. With
(80) other black boys the strife was not so fiercely sunny: their youth shrunk into tasteless sycophancy, or into silent hatred of the pale world about them and mocking distrust of everything white; or wasted itself in a bitter cry, Why did God make me an outcast and a stranger in my own house? The
(85) shades of the prison-house closed round about us all: walls strait and stubborn to the whitest, but relentlessly narrow, tall, and unscalable to sons of night who must plod darkly on in resignation, or beat unavailing palms against the stone, or steadily, half hopelessly, watch the streak of blue above.

1. In Passage 1, the two incidents recounted by Douglass primarily illustrate
   (A) Douglass's intelligence and wit
   (B) the kindness of well-educated white Northerners
   (C) small victories over the segregation of African-Americans from whites
   (D) the difference between post-Civil War society in the South and in the North
   (E) the bitterness of whites toward African-Americans after the Civil War

2. The term "barroom loafers" (line 5) suggests that
   (A) Douglass had contempt for white people
   (B) the attitudes of the people in the bar were different from the attitudes of most white Northerners
   (C) the people in the bar were drunkards
   (D) the employment situation in Janesville was poor
   (E) the people were regular customers at the bar

3. At dinner on the lake steamer, Douglass waited for the second table in order to
   - (A) sit next to someone he knew would be a gentleman
   - (B) make a statement against the separation of African-Americans from whites
   - (C) avoid clashing with the "rough element" on board
   - (D) prove his ability to fight the ship's steward
   - (E) act as a role model to his "sable brethren" by refusing to be intimidated

4. Passage 1 implies all of the following about the author EXCEPT:
   - (A) He was known by influential whites.
   - (B) He appreciated intelligence and good manners.
   - (C) He responded to provocation but didn't initiate it.
   - (D) He did not believe in physical fighting.
   - (E) He had a sense of humor.

5. Which of the following is the best example of Douglass's irony in Passage 1?
   - (A) ". . . the horses of Janesville were more civilized than its people" (lines 11-12)
   - (B) "It was not to be trifled with, especially when hungry" (lines 18-19)
   - (C) "His whole appearance told me he was *somebody*" (line 26)
   - (D) "Before my sable brethren could execute their captain's order . . ." (lines 37-38)
   - (E) "Let the gentleman alone! I am not ashamed to take my tea with Mr. Douglass" (lines 40-42)

6. In Passage 2, the "other world" in line 44 refers to
    (A) America as opposed to Europe
    (B) educated white people as opposed to uneducated African-Americans
    (C) American Southerners as opposed to American Northerners
    (D) white Americans as opposed to African-Americans
    (E) people who believed in segregation as opposed to those who believed in integration

7. In the first paragraph of Passage 2, Du Bois's response to the comments and questions he receives can best be described as
    (A) angry and argumentative
    (B) learned and philosophical
    (C) polite but incomplete
    (D) cruel but accurate
    (E) mocking and misleading

8. Based on information in Passage 2, what is the most likely reason that the author answers "seldom a word" to "the real question" (lines 54-55)?
    (A) People don't listen when he tries to answer.
    (B) Those who ask the question would use the answer against him.
    (C) If he answered the question truthfully, he would be persecuted by those who asked it.
    (D) Experiencing the answer is the only possible way to begin to understand it.
    (E) The question itself is a sign of prejudice, and any answer would be irrelevant.

9. The best definition for "peremptorily" in line 65 is
    (A) decisively, without thinking twice
    (B) snobbishly
    (C) politely but condescendingly
    (D) angrily
    (E) with mockery and disdain

10. When Du Bois first recognizes he is "different from the others" (line 66), he feels
    (A) contempt for himself
    (B) contempt for "the others"
    (C) longing and envy
    (D) humiliation and fury
    (E) hopelessness and depression

11. The implication of lines 71-79 is that Du Bois
    (A) despised whites and their achievements
    (B) was motivated to achieve chiefly by a desire to help less fortunate African-Americans
    (C) was more intelligent than both his white and African-American "mates"
    (D) was spurred to achievement by competitiveness with whites
    (E) desired revenge for wrongs that had been done to him

12. The author of Passage 2 describes his strife as "fiercely sunny" (line 80) to
    (A) indicate his hatred
    (B) emphasize both his determination and his positive attitude
    (C) ironically comment on his efforts to achieve
    (D) ridicule African-Americans who resorted to "tasteless sycophancy"
    (E) mock the stereotype of the "happy slave"

13. "The prison-house" in line 85 most likely refers to
    (A) slavery
    (B) school
    (C) the world
    (D) hatred
    (E) a sense of hopelessness

14. Which one of the following statements applies to both Passage 1
    and Passage 2?
    (A) Both passages are about how separation of African-Americans
        from the white community affects children.
    (B) Both authors imply that Northerners understood African-
        Americans better than Southerners did.
    (C) In both passages inferior education is shown to be the key
        reason African-Americans are not accepted by whites.
    (D) Both authors use personal experiences to make a point.
    (E) In both passages the authors advocate civil disobedience for
        African-Americans.

15. All of the following statements correctly contrast the two pas-
    sages EXCEPT:
    (A) The emphasis in Passage 1 is on external events, while the
        emphasis in Passage 2 is on internal reactions.
    (B) Passage 2 uses several figures of speech and images to
        make a point, while Passage 1 uses none.
    (C) Passage 1 presents a more positive picture of a white per-
        son than does Passage 2.
    (D) Passage 2 is more dramatic and uses more rhetorical
        devices than Passage 1.
    (E) While the author of Passage 1 is a static character and nar-
        rator, the author of Passage 2 presents himself as a devel-
        oping character.

STOP. IF YOU FINISH BEFORE TIME IS CALLED, CHECK
YOUR WORK ON THIS SECTION ONLY. DO NOT WORK ON
ANY OTHER SECTION IN THE TEST.

Time: 30 Minutes
25 Questions

DIRECTIONS

Solve each problem in this section by using the information given and your own mathematical calculations, insights, and problem-solving skills. Then select the one correct answer of the five choices given and mark the corresponding circle on your answer sheet. Use the available space on the page for your scratch work.

Notes

(1) All numbers used are real numbers.

(2) Calculators may be used.

(3) Some problems may be accompanied by figures or diagrams. These figures are drawn as accurately as possible EXCEPT when it is stated in a specific problem that a figure is not drawn to scale. The figures and diagrams are meant to provide information useful in solving the problem or problems. Unless otherwise stated, all figures and diagrams lie in a plane.

Data That May Be Used for Reference

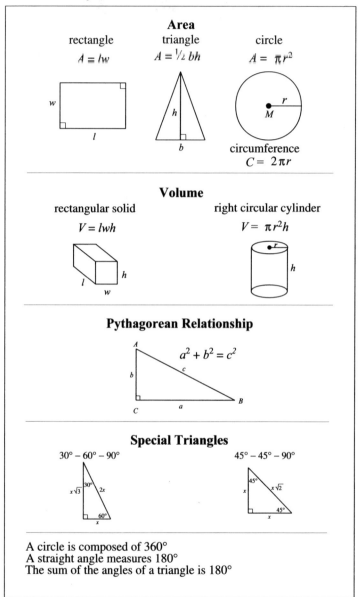

Area

rectangle

$A = lw$

triangle

$A = \frac{1}{2}bh$

circle

$A = \pi r^2$

circumference

$C = 2\pi r$

Volume

rectangular solid

$V = lwh$

right circular cylinder

$V = \pi r^2 h$

Pythagorean Relationship

$a^2 + b^2 = c^2$

Special Triangles

$30° - 60° - 90°$

$45° - 45° - 90°$

A circle is composed of 360°
A straight angle measures 180°
The sum of the angles of a triangle is 180°

1. If $(p-q) = 2^2$, what is the value of $[2(p-q)]^2$?
   (A) 4　　(B) 8　　(C) 16　　(D) 32　　(E) 64

2. Raul spent one third of his pocket money on a video game and the remaining $6 on a music tape. What was the total amount of Raul's pocket money?
   (A) $3　　(B) $4　　(C) $6　　(D) $9　　(E) $12

3. If $\dfrac{a}{b} = \dfrac{c}{d}$ and $\dfrac{d}{c} = \dfrac{4}{3}$, which of the following is the value of $\left(\dfrac{a}{b}\right)^2$?

   (A) $\frac{9}{16}$　　(B) $\frac{3}{4}$　　(C) $\frac{4}{3}$　　(D) $\frac{3}{2}$　　(E) $\frac{16}{9}$

4. If 3 is the product of $\frac{1}{3}$ and x, what is the sum of $\frac{1}{3}$ and x?
   (A) $\frac{1}{3}$　　(B) 1　　(C) $1\frac{1}{3}$　　(D) 3　　(E) $9\frac{1}{3}$

5. If 30 is 15% of x, what is x?
   (A) 34.5　　(B) 100　　(C) 150　　(D) 200　　(E) 450

6. Barry is 20 years older than Al. In 10 years, Barry will be twice Al's age then. What is Barry's current age in years?
   (A) 20　　(B) 30　　(C) 40　　(D) 50　　(E) 60

7. Distance AB, as measured by an inaccurate tape measure is $\frac{1}{2}$ mile. For every 11 inches, the tape measure reads 12 inches. What is the correct length of AB? (1 mile = 5,280 feet)
   (A) $\frac{1}{2}$ mile − 440 feet
   (B) $\frac{1}{2}$ mile − 220 feet
   (C) $\frac{1}{2}$ mile − 20 feet
   (D) $\frac{1}{2}$ mile + 220 feet
   (E) $\frac{1}{2}$ mile + 440 feet

8. What is the maximum number of squares, each of side 4 inches, that can be cut from a square sheet of paper of side 14 inches?
   (A) 9   (B) 10   (C) 11   (D) 12   (E) 13

9. If $7x + 14y = 35$, what is the value of $2x + 4y$?
   (A) 10   (B) 21   (C) 25   (D) 28   (E) 56

10. If the length of a rectangle is 1.5 times its width and the perimeter of the rectangle is 20, what is the area of the rectangle?
    (A) 10   (B) 20   (C) 24   (D) 37.5   (E) 40

Questions 11-12 refer to the chart below, which shows the weekly earnings of employees in Company X according to the number of hours worked per week.

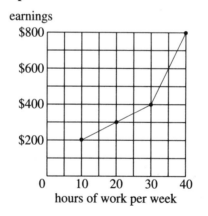

11. If Company X employs 20 people who work 20 hours per week, 5 people who work 30 hours per week, and 5 people who work 40 hours per week, what is the total of the weekly earnings of these 30 employees?
    (A) $750
    (B) $6,200
    (C) $7,500
    (D) $8,000
    (E) $12,000

12. According to the chart, the earnings of a person who works 40 hours per week is approximately what percent of the earnings of a person who works 10 hours per week?

    (A) 400   (B) 300   (C) 200   (D) 100   (E) 50

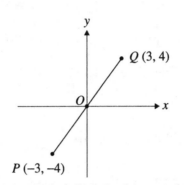

13. In the figure above, a circle is to be drawn such that PQ passes through the origin and is the circle's diameter. Which of the following points will lie on the circle?

    (A) (3, 0)   (B) (5, 0)   (C) (0, 4)   (D) (0, 3)   (E) (5, 5)

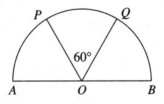

14. In the figure above, arc $APQB$ is a semicircle of length 60π inches. What is the length of arc PQ in inches?

    (A) 10π (B) 20π (C) 30π (D) 40π (E) 50π

15. Elaine has only 7 pennies, some nickels, and some dimes in her purse. If she has a total of 14 coins that add up to 62 cents, how many dimes does she have?

    (A) 1   (B) 2   (C) 3   (D) 4   (E) 5

16. The meter in a taxicab registers $2.00 for the first mile and $0.40 for each additional half mile. The price registered by the meter for a trip 6 miles long is how many times greater than the price registered by the meter for a trip 3 miles long?
    (A) $\frac{3}{5}$ (B) $\frac{10}{7}$ (C) $\frac{5}{3}$ (D) $\frac{5}{2}$ (E) 2

17. When a strip of paper is cut into two smaller strips whose lengths are in the ratio 2 : 3, the length of one strip exceeds the length of the other by exactly 6 inches. What was the length of the paper, in inches, before it was cut?
    (A) 6   (B) 12   (C) 18   (D) 20   (E) 30

18. Which of the following must be true about a set of six consecutive even integers?

    I. The set contains only one number that is divisible by 5.
    II. Exactly two numbers in the set are divisible by 3.
    III. Exactly three numbers in the set are divisible by 4.

    (A) I only
    (B) II only
    (C) I and II only
    (D) II and III only
    (E) I, II, and III

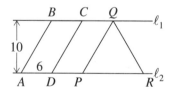

19. In the figure above, line ℓ_1 is parallel to line ℓ_2, the distance between them is 10, and AD is 6. If the area of the parallelogram $ABCD$ is equal to the area of triangle PQR, what is the length of PR?
    (A) 6   (B) 9   (C) 10   (D) 12   (E) 18

20. If ##*x*## denotes a circle of area *x,* what is the circumference of the circle denoted by ##5##?

(A) $2\sqrt{5\pi}$ (B) 5   (C) $\dfrac{10}{\pi}$ (D) $\dfrac{5}{\pi}$ (E) $2\sqrt{\dfrac{5}{\pi^3}}$

Number of People	Position	Weekly Wage per Person
3	administrator	$500
2	engineer	$1,000
2	sales agent	$800
1	assistant manager	$1,500
1	manager	$2,500

21. The weekly wages received by all nine employees in a company were as shown in the table above. If two of the administrators quit their jobs, the median weekly wage in the company with seven employees is what percent of the median weekly wage when all nine employees were in the company?

(A) 25   (B) 80   (C) 120   (D) 125   (E) 180

22. A square sheet of paper of side 10 inches is folded in half. This rectangular sheet is again folded in half so that the resulting shape is a square of side 5 inches. If a circular hole of radius 2 inches is cut through the center of this square and the sheet of paper is unfolded back to a square of side 10 inches, what is the area of the sheet of paper, in square inches, that is NOT cut?

(A) $8\pi - 100$

(B) $16\pi - 100$

(C) $100 - 16\pi$

(D) $100 - 8\pi$

(E) $100 - 4\pi$

23. A set contains n consecutive even positive integers, and

$$s = \frac{\text{the sum of all members in the set}}{n}$$

If $n = 2k$, where k is a positive integer, which of the following must be true about s?

I. s is an even number.
II. s is an odd number.
III. s is less than n.

(A) I only
(B) II only
(C) III only
(D) I and III only
(E) II and III only

24. An ant is crawling up a tree that is 30 feet tall. In the daytime, the ant gains 3 feet, but at night, it drops 2 feet. If, on the morning of January 1, the ant begins its climb from the bottom of the tree, when will it first reach the top of the tree?
(A) January 27
(B) January 28
(C) January 29
(D) January 30
(E) January 31

25. A set has four numbers. The median of the four numbers is 7, the average (arithmetic mean) of the four numbers is 8, and the greatest number in the set is 14. If the average of the two smallest numbers in the set is 5, what is the smallest number in the set?
(A) 4   (B) 5   (C) 6   (D) 7   (E) 8

STOP. IF YOU FINISH BEFORE TIME IS CALLED, CHECK YOUR WORK ON THIS SECTION ONLY. DO NOT WORK ON ANY OTHER SECTION IN THE TEST.

SCORING AND COMPLETE ANSWERS AND EXPLANATIONS FOR THE PRACTICE TEST

Answer Key

Section 1 Mathematical Reasoning	Section 2 Verbal Reasoning		Section 3 Mathematical Reasoning
1. B	1. E	26. C	1. C
2. C	2. D	27. A	2. B
3. E	3. A	28. C	3. C
4. D	4. A	29. D	4. B
5. C	5. C	30. E	5. A
6. D	6. C	31. C	6. A
7. E	7. E		7. C
8. D	8. E		8. D
9. C	9. B		9. B
10. D	10. C		10. A
11. D	11. A		11. B
12. B	12. E		12. B
13. E	13. D		13. D
14. D	14. D		14. A
15. A	15. D		15. A
16. D	16. B		16. 45
17. A	17. D		17. 30
18. A	18. C		18. $\frac{20}{6}$ or $\frac{10}{3}$ or 3.33
19. B	19. A		19. 80
20. B	20. C		20. 99
21. E	21. E		21. 2,340
22. B	22. B		22. 16
23. D	23. C		23. 8
24. B	24. A		24. 4
25. B	25. E		25. 4

Section 4
Verbal
Reasoning

1. C	26. D
2. B	27. B
3. C	28. C
4. A	29. D
5. D	30. C
6. E	31. D
7. B	32. C
8. D	33. A
9. B	34. C
10. E	35. C
11. B	
12. E	
13. B	
14. E	
15. C	
16. D	
17. B	
18. A	
19. B	
20. A	
21. C	
22. E	
23. C	
24. B	
25. A	

Section 5
Mathematical
Reasoning

1. B
2. B
3. C
4. B
5. A
6. D
7. D
8. C
9. C
10. D

Section 6
Verbal
Reasoning

1. C
2. E
3. C
4. D
5. A
6. D
7. C
8. D
9. A
10. B
11. D
12. B
13. C
14. D
15. B

Section 7
Mathematical
Reasoning

1. E
2. D
3. A
4. E
5. D
6. B
7. B
8. A
9. A
10. C
11. E
12. A
13. B
14. B
15. D
16. C
17. E
18. D
19. D
20. A
21. D
22. C
23. B
24. B
25. A

Analyzing Your Test Results

Use the charts on the following pages to carefully analyze your results and to spot your strengths and weaknesses. Completely analyze each subject area and each individual problem in the practice test. Then reexamine the results for trends in types of errors (repeated errors) or poor results in specific subject areas. **This reexamination and analysis is of tremendous importance in assuring your maximum test preparation benefit.**

Verbal Reasoning Analysis Sheet

Section 2	**possible**	**completed**	**right**	**wrong**
sentence completion	9			
analogies	6			
critical reading	16			
Subtotal	31			

Section 4	**possible**	**completed**	**right**	**wrong**
sentence completion	10			
analogies	13			
critical reading	12			
Subtotal	35			

Section 6	**possible**	**completed**	**right**	**wrong**
critical reading	15			
Subtotal	15			

Overall Verbal Totals	81			

Mathematical Reasoning Analysis Sheet

Section 1

	possible	completed	right	wrong
multiple choice	25			
Subtotal	25			

Section 3

	possible	completed	right	wrong
quantitative comparison	15			
grid-ins	10			
Subtotal	25			

Section 5

	possible	completed	right	wrong
multiple choice	10			
Subtotal	10			

Section 7

	possible	completed	right	wrong
multiple choice	25			
Subtotal	25			

Overall Math Totals	85			

You can now use the tables on page 10 to convert your raw scores to an **approximate** scaled score.

Analysis/Tally Sheet for Problems Missed

One of the most important parts of test preparation is analyzing **why** you missed a problem so that you can reduce the number of mistakes. Now that you've taken the practice test and checked your answers, carefully tally your mistakes by marking them in the proper column.

Reason for Mistakes

	total missed	simple mistake	misread problem	lack of knowledge	lack of time
Section 2: verbal					
Section 4: verbal					
Section 6: verbal					
Subtotal					
Section 1: math					
Section 3: math					
Section 5: math					
Section 7: math					
Subtotal					
Total Math and Verbal					

Reviewing the above data should help you determine **why** you're missing certain problems. Now that you've pinpointed the type of error, you'll be aware that you must focus on avoiding that type of error on the actual test.

1. (B) Because the capacity of each sack is given in pounds (not in kilograms), you should first convert the total weight (20 kilograms) into pounds. You're given that 1 kilogram is 2.25 pounds. Then

$$20 \text{ kilograms} = 2.25 \times 20$$
$$= 45 \text{ pounds}$$

(Notice that to mentally multiply 2.25 by 20, first multiply 2.25 by 10, which can be done by moving the decimal one place to the right, to get 22.5, and then multiply 22.5 by 2 to get 45.)

If the total is 45 pounds and each sack can hold 9 pounds, then the number of sacks required is $45 \div 9$, which is 5. *Using your calculator could save you time on this problem.*

2. (C) If $y + 2$ is positive, it means that $y + 2$ must be greater than zero. That is,

$$y + 2 > 0$$
$$y > -2$$

That is, y is greater than -2.

3. (E) The quantity within the parentheses $(7 + r - 4)$ can be simplified to $(3 + r)$. Then

$$-5(3 + r) = -30$$
$$-15 - 5r = -30$$

Adding 15 to both sides, you get

$$-5r = -15$$

Dividing both sides by –5,

$$\frac{-5r}{-5} = \frac{-15}{-5}$$

So $r = 3$.

4. (D) Notice that p is not divisible by 3, 4, or 5 (because there is always a remainder when p is divided by these numbers), which means that your answer cannot be divisible by 3, 4, or 5. Working from the answers, you can rule out answer choices (A) 12 (because it is divisible by both 3 and 4) and (C) 20 (because it is divisible by both 4 and 5). Now you're left with choices (B), (D), and (E).

If choice (B) 14 is divided by 3, the remainder is 2 (because $14 \div 3$ is 4 with remainder 2). But when it is divided by 4, the remainder is also 2 (not 1). Therefore, choice (B) cannot be the correct answer.

If choice (D) 29 is divided by 3, the remainder is 2. If it is divided by 4, the remainder is 1, and if it is divided by 5, the remainder is 4. So choice (D) is the correct answer.

5. (C) The area of a triangle is $\frac{1}{2} \times$ base $\times$ height.

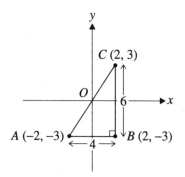

Base *AB* of the triangle is 4 units (because from *A* to the *y*-axis is 2 units and from the *y*-axis to *B* is another 2 units). Height *BC* of the triangle is 6 units (3 units from *B* to the *x*-axis and another 3 units to *C*). Note that $\angle B$ is a right angle. So

$$\text{area of triangle} = \tfrac{1}{2} \times 4 \times 6$$
$$= \tfrac{1}{2} \times 24$$
$$= 12$$

6. (D) You may wish to sketch a figure.

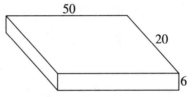

The volume of the swimming pool is equal to its length × width × depth. The volume of the swimming pool is also the volume of the water needed to completely fill the swimming pool. Then

$$\text{volume of water} = 50 \times 20 \times 6$$
$$= 1{,}000 \times 6$$
$$= 6{,}000 \text{ cubic feet}$$

Since each cubic foot of water costs 30 cents ($0.30),

$$\text{total cost} = .30 \times 6{,}000$$
$$= \$1{,}800$$

7. (E) In the formula for the area of a circle (area $= \pi r^2$), the radius is squared. So if the radius is multiplied by 3, the area will be increased by 3^2, or 9 times.

Another way to solve this problem is to plug in your own values. Assume that the initial radius is 2. Then

$$\text{area of circle} = \pi r^2$$
$$= \pi(2)^2$$
$$= 4\pi$$

Now, if the radius is multiplied by 3, the new radius is $3 \times 2 = 6$. So

$$\text{area of new circle} = \pi r^2$$
$$= \pi(6)^2$$
$$= 36\pi$$

The second area (36π) is 9 times the first area (4π).

8. (D) Constructing a simple chart may be the fastest method to answer this question. The chart would look something like this.

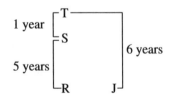

The answer can be derived from this chart; only I and II must be true. You could also work the problem mathematically, like this.

Since Sue is 5 years older than Roberta, you can write

$$S = R + 5$$

And since Tim is 6 years older than John,

$$T = J + 6$$

You also know that Tim is 1 year older than Sue. That is,

$$T = S + 1$$

From the first equation, you know that $S = R + 5$. You can substitute this value of S in the third equation. Then

$$T = S + 1 = R + 5 + 1$$
$$T = S + 1 = R + 6$$

You also know that $T = J + 6$. So you can write

$$T = S + 1 = R + 6 = J + 6$$

Now you can use an elimination strategy by looking at the roman numerals. Numeral I says that Tim is 6 years older than Roberta, which is true because $T = R + 6$. So roman numeral I must be true. At this point, knock out any answer choice that doesn't have roman numeral I in it—in this case, choices (B) and (C). You're left with choices (A), (D), and (E).

Roman numeral II says that John and Roberta are the same age. The last part of the equation above is $R + 6 = J + 6$. If you subtract 6 from both sides of this equation, you get $R=J$. So roman numeral II is also true. Again, knock out any answer choice that doesn't have roman numeral II in it. You can now knock out choice (A), and you're left with only choices (D) and (E) as possibilities.

Roman numeral III says that Sue is 7 years older than John. From the equation above, you see that

$$S + 1 = J + 6$$
$$S = J + 5$$

So Sue is 5 years older than John, not 7, and roman numeral III is false. Since you can knock out choice (E), the right answer is choice (D).

9. (C) To find the time when the toys will beep together again, you need to find the common multiple of 8, 10, and 12. To find the common multiple, take the greatest of the three numbers, 12, and find its multiple that is also a multiple of the other two.

Multiples of 12 are 12, 24, 36, 48, 60, 72, 84, 96, 108, and 120. Notice that 120 is the first multiple of 12 that is also a multiple of both 8 (because $8 \times 15 = 120$) and 10 ($10 \times 12 = 120$). So the toys will next beep together after 120 minutes, that is, after 2 hours. Two hours after 1:00 a.m. is 3:00 a.m.

10. (D) To find the perimeter of the triangle, you need the lengths of the three sides. You know that radius OB is 3 units long. Then OA and OC are each 3 units because they are also radii. Therefore, side AC of the triangle is 6 units.

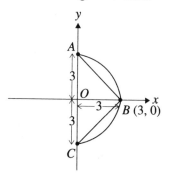

In triangle *AOB,* you know that *OA* is 3 and *OB* is 3. From the Pythagorean theorem,

$$a^2 + b^2 = c^2$$
$$(OA)^2 + (OB)^2 = (AB)^2$$
$$3^2 + 3^2 = (AB)^2$$
$$9 + 9 = (AB)^2$$
$$18 = (AB)^2$$
$$\sqrt{18} = AB$$
$$\sqrt{9 \times 2} = AB$$
$$3\sqrt{2} = AB$$

(If you spotted that triangle *AOB* is an isosceles right triangle with sides in the ratio $1:1:\sqrt{2}$, you wouldn't have needed to use the Pythagorean theorem.)

By symmetry, you know that $AB = CB$. So $CB = 3\sqrt{2}$ and

$$\text{perimeter} = CA + AB + CB$$
$$= 6 + 3\sqrt{2} + 3\sqrt{2}$$
$$= 6 + 6\sqrt{2}$$

11. (D) Numbers that are divisible by both 4 and 6 are 12, 24, 36, and so forth. Don't forget that *d* can be a negative number as well. For example, -12, -24, and -36 are all divisible by both 4 and 6.

To answer this question, you might want to use an elimination strategy. Because *d* can be either positive or negative, you can rule out roman numeral III, which says that *d* must be greater than 0. That is, roman numeral III cannot be a part of the final answer. At this point, you can knock out choices (C) and (E) because each one contains roman numeral III. So you're left with choices (A), (B), and (D).

Because *d* is divisible by 6, *d* must also be divisible by 3. So roman numeral I must be part of the answer. At this point, you can rule out choice (B) because it doesn't have roman numeral I.

Roman numeral II says that *d* must be a multiple of 12. If *d* is divisible by both 4 and 6, the smallest positive value for *d* must be 12 because no other smaller positive number is divisible by both 4 and 6. The next greater number is 24, which is another multiple of 12. (In problems like this, take the greater of the two numbers—in this case, 6—and think about its multiples, for example, 6, 12, 18, and 24. Of these numbers, you'll see that only 12 and 24 are divisible by both 4 and 6.) So roman numeral II must also be true, which means that both I and II must be part of the answer. So (D) is the right answer.

12. **(B)** In $\triangle ABC$, $\angle A$ is $30°$ and $\angle C$ is $90°$. Then

$$\angle B = 180° - (\angle A + \angle C)$$
$$= 180 - (30 + 90)$$
$$= 180 - 120$$
$$= 60°$$

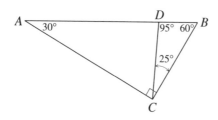

In the smaller triangle, $\triangle BDC$, you see that

$$\angle D = 95°$$
$$\angle B = 60°$$

So

$$\angle D + \angle B = 95 + 60$$
$$= 155$$

Then $\angle x$ must be $180 - 155 = 25°$.

13. (E) Plug in your own values for x and n. If x is a negative number (say, -2) and n is a prime number (say, 3), then the value of p is

$$(-2)^3 = -2 \times -2 \times -2 = -8$$

So choice (A) is incorrect; p is not necessarily a positive number.

And p is not greater than 1 if x is a fraction (say $\frac{1}{2}$). If x is $\frac{1}{2}$ and n is 3, then p is $\left(\frac{1}{2}\right)^3 = \frac{1}{8}$. So choice (B) is also incorrect; p is not necessarily greater than 1.

If x is 2 and n is 3, then p is $2^3 = 8$, which is not prime. Choice (C) is also incorrect.

If x is 3 and n is 3, then p is $p = 2^3 = 8$, which is not an even number. Choice (D) is also incorrect.

Because all prime numbers are also whole numbers, notice that any whole-number power of x will always be a multiple of x. That is, if x is 2 and n is 3, then $p = 2^3 = 8$, which is a multiple of 2. This is true even if x is a fraction (say, $\frac{1}{2}$). Then $p = \left(\frac{1}{2}\right)^3 = \frac{1}{8}$, which is also a multiple of $\frac{1}{2}$.

14. (D) You know that there are 20 Japanese cars in the lot and that this number represents 10% of all cars in the lot. If 20 is 10% of the total, then the total (which is 100%) must be

$$20 \times 10 = 200 \text{ cars}$$

If the total number of cars in the lot is 200, then
American cars + Japanese cars + European cars = 200

$$60 + 20 + E = 200$$
$$80 + E = 200$$
$$E = 200 - 80$$
$$E = 120$$

15. (A) You need to find the value of

$$\frac{AB}{C}, \text{ which can be written as } AB \times \frac{1}{C}$$

Then

$$\frac{AB}{C} = AB \times \frac{1}{C}$$

$$= \frac{p}{q} \times \frac{q^2}{r} \times \frac{1}{\frac{s}{r^2}}$$

Since

$$\frac{1}{\frac{s}{r^2}} = \frac{r^2}{s}$$

Then

$$AB \times \frac{1}{C} = \frac{p}{q} \times \frac{q^2}{r} \times \frac{r^2}{s}$$

Canceling gives

$$AB \times \frac{1}{C} = \frac{p}{\cancel{q}} \times \frac{q^{\cancel{2}^1}}{\cancel{r}} \times \frac{r^{\cancel{2}^1}}{s} = \frac{pqr}{s}$$

16. (D) If you roll the sheet of paper as shown in the diagram, you will get a cylinder of height 8.

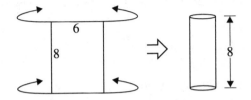

To find the volume of the cylinder, you need to first find the radius of the cylinder. Since the width of the sheet of paper is 6, the circumference of the cylinder will also be 6. (If you had rolled the sheet of paper around its length, its circumference would have been 8.) If the circumference of the cylinder is 6, then you can find its radius using the formula $C = 2\pi r$. That is,

$$C = 2\pi r$$
$$6 = 2\pi r$$

Dividing each side by 2π,

$$\frac{\cancel{6}^{\ 3}}{\cancel{2}\pi} = \frac{\cancel{2}\cancel{\pi}r}{\cancel{2}\cancel{\pi}}$$

$$\frac{3}{\pi} = r$$

The volume of the cylinder is, where h is the height, 8, and $r = \dfrac{3}{\pi}$,

$$V = \pi r^2 h$$

$$= \frac{\cancel{\pi}}{1} \times \frac{3}{\cancel{\pi}} \times \frac{3}{\pi} \times \frac{8}{1}$$

$$= \frac{72}{\pi}$$

17. (A) Let a, b, and c be the three numbers in the set, from least to greatest, respectively. Then c must be 5 (because you're told that the greatest number is 5). The average of the two smallest numbers is

$$\frac{a+b}{2}$$

You're told that this average is 5 less than the average of all three numbers in the set. The average of all three numbers is

$$\frac{a+b+5}{3}$$

Then you can form the equation

$$\frac{a+b}{2} = \frac{a+b+5}{3} - 5$$

Multiplying both sides of the equation by 6 (a multiple of both 2 and 3, to eliminate the denominators), you get

$$\frac{\cancel{6}^{3}}{1} \times \frac{a+b}{\cancel{2}} = \left(\frac{\cancel{6}^{2}}{1} \times \frac{a+b+5}{\cancel{3}} \right) - \left(\frac{6}{1} \times \frac{5}{1} \right)$$

$$3(a+b) = 2(a+b+5) - 30$$
$$3a + 3b = 2a + 2b + 10 - 30$$
$$3a + 3b = 2a + 2b - 20$$

Subtract $2a + 2b$ from each side, which leaves
$$a+b = -20$$

Since $a + b$ is the sum of the two smallest numbers, their sum is -20. In this problem, you could also work from the answers.

18. (A) Because Ralph kept the car for 6 days, his daily rate was $30. Furthermore, he paid for only 5 days. So the total amount he paid was

$$5 \times 30 = \$150$$

Because he actually kept the car for 6 days, his daily rate was

$$150 \div 6 = \$25$$

Bill had to pay $40 per day. So his average daily rate was $40. So the average daily rate paid by Ralph is

$$\frac{25}{40} \times 100 = 62.5\%$$

of that paid by Bill.

19. (B) In $\triangle ABC$, $\angle B$ is a right angle and AB and BC are equal. (Note that you are told that this figure is not drawn to scale, and consequently, you must ignore the fact that AB and BC or AE and EC may not appear to be equal.) Then using the Pythagorean theorem,

$$c^2 = a^2 + b^2$$
$$(AC)^2 = (AB)^2 + (BC)^2$$
$$= \left(\sqrt{2}\right)^2 + \left(\sqrt{2}\right)^2$$
$$= 2 + 2$$
$$(AC)^2 = 4$$
$$AC = 2$$

You're told that $AC = AD$, so $AD = 2$.

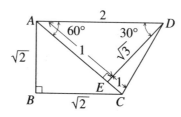

Right triangle *AED* has a 60° angle, which means that ∠*EDA* must be 30° that is, △*AED* is a 30°– 60°– 90° triangle. You know that a 30°– 60°– 90° triangle has sides in the ratio $1, \sqrt{3}$, and 2, respectively. You know that side *AD*, which is opposite the 90° angle, is 2. So side *AE*, which is opposite the 30° angle, must be 1, and side *ED*, which is opposite the 60° angle, must be $\sqrt{3}$. Also, because *AC* = 2, and *AE* = 1, then *EC* must be 2 – 1 = 1.

Now, to find the area of △*DEC* because you know the height, *ED* = $\sqrt{3}$, and you know the base, *EC* = 1, then

$$\text{area of } \triangle DEC = \tfrac{1}{2} \times \text{base} \times \text{height}$$

$$= \tfrac{1}{2} \times 1 \times \sqrt{3}$$

$$= \frac{\sqrt{3}}{2}$$

20. (B) First simplify the equation by multiplying $(x + 4)(x + 1)$.

$$(x + 4)(x + 1) = x^2 + 4x + 1x + 4$$

$$= x^2 + 5x + 4$$

Next multiply $(x - 5)(x - 2)$.

$$(x - 5)(x - 2) = x^2 - 5x - 2x + 10$$

$$= x^2 - 7x + 10$$

Now take a negative of the second expression because in the original equation there is a negative sign in front of it. This operation leaves

$$-x^2 + 7x - 10$$

The original equation now looks like this.

$$x^2 + 5x + 4 - x^2 + 7x - 10 = 0$$

Simplifying the left side by combining like terms leaves

$$12x - 6 = 0$$

Adding 6 to each side gives

$$12x = 6$$
$$x = \frac{6}{12}$$
$$x = \frac{1}{2}$$

But the question asks for the value of $x^2 - x$, which is

$$\left(\frac{1}{2}\right)^2 - \frac{1}{2} = \frac{1}{4} - \frac{1}{2}$$
$$= -\frac{1}{4}$$

21. (E) You know that

$$j = 5*$$
$$= 5 + \text{the lowest prime number} > 5$$
$$= 5 + 7 \text{ (because } 7 = \text{ the lowest prime number} > 5)$$
$$= 12$$

You now need to find $j*$. Then

$$j* = 12 + \text{ the lowest prime number} > 12$$
$$= 12 + 13$$
$$= 25$$

22. (B) If $d - 2$ is the length and $d - 5$ is the width, then the area of the photograph is length × width.

$$\text{area} = (d - 2)(d - 5)$$
$$= d^2 - 7d + 10$$

But you know that the area is 40. So

$$40 = d^2 - 7d + 10$$
$$0 = d^2 - 7d - 30$$

Factoring gives

$$0 = (d - 10)(d + 3)$$

Setting each one equal to 0,

$$0 = d - 10$$
$$0 = d + 3$$

From this equation, d can be either -3 or 10. But since d can't be negative, d has to be 10. If d is 10, then the width is

$$d - 5 = 5$$

For this problem, working from the answers is also efficient. If you start from the middle answer (C),

If the width $(d - 5)$ is 8, then the length $(d - 2)$ is 11. Does $8 \times 11 = 40$? No. (C) is incorrect; $8 \times 11 = 88$, a value that is too high, so try (B).

If the width $(d - 5)$ is 5, then the length $(d - 2)$ is 8. Does $5 \times 8 = 40$? Yes. So (B) is correct, and you need go no farther.

23. (D) One way to solve this problem is to plug in the answers. Start from choice (C) 360. If the distance between the two towns is 360 miles, then, traveling at 40 miles per hour, Manuel would have taken $\frac{360}{40} = 9$ hours and $\frac{360}{60} = 6$ hours, for a total of hours. This is too low because you're told that the entire trip took him 20 hours. Since, as you can see, 360 is too low, you can knock out choice (C). If choice (C) is too low, so are choices (A) and (B). So the answer has to be either choice (D) or choice (E).

Now try choice (D) 480. If the distance is 480, then the trip to Bayville would have lasted $\frac{480}{40} = 12$ hours, and the return trip would have lasted $\frac{480}{60} = 8$ hours, for a total of 20 hours. So (D) is the right answer.

Another way of solving this problem is to assume that it took Manuel x hours to make the trip to Bayville. Then the distance from Albertville to Bayville is $40(x)$ (because distance = speed × time). If the total time is 20 hours, then the return trip must have lasted $20 - x$ hours. So the distance from Bayville to Albertville must be

$$60(20 - x) = 1,200 - 60x$$

But the two distances are equal. So

$$40x = 1,200 - 60x$$
$$40x + 60x = 1,200$$
$$100x = 1,200$$
$$x = 12$$

If $x = 12$, the distance from Albertville to Bayville is
$$40 \times 12 = 480 \text{ miles}$$

24. (B) If x represents the total value of the estate, then $\frac{3}{4}x$ represents the amount that was distributed among the charities. Because four charities received equal amounts,

$$\text{amount received by each charity} = \frac{3}{4}x \div 4$$
$$= \frac{3x}{4} \times \frac{1}{4}$$
$$= \frac{3x}{16}$$

You know that each charity spent $\frac{3}{4}$ of the amount it received. That is,

$$\text{amount spent by each charity} = \frac{3}{4} \times \frac{3x}{16}$$
$$= \frac{9x}{64}$$

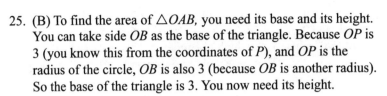

25. (B) To find the area of △*OAB*, you need its base and its height. You can take side *OB* as the base of the triangle. Because *OP* is 3 (you know this from the coordinates of *P*), and *OP* is the radius of the circle, *OB* is also 3 (because *OB* is another radius). So the base of the triangle is 3. You now need its height.

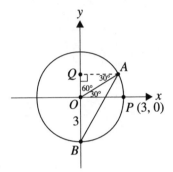

To find the height of the triangle, you can project its base *OB* to point *Q*. Then *AQ* is the height of the triangle. Note that because ∠*AOP* is 30°, ∠*QOA* must be 90° − 30° = 60°. And because *OA* is also a radius, it is 3. So now you have △*OQA* a 30° − 60° − 90° right triangle in which

$$\angle AQO = 90°$$
$$\angle QOA = 60°$$
$$\angle OAQ = 30°$$

In a triangle, the three corresponding sides are in the ratio 1, $\sqrt{3}$, and 2, respectively. In $\triangle OAQ$, side OA, which is opposite the $90°$ angle, is 3, which is $\frac{3}{2}$ times 2. Then side AQ, which is opposite the $60°$ angle, should be $\frac{3}{2}$ times $\sqrt{3}$. That is, the height of $\triangle OAB$ is $\frac{3}{2}\sqrt{3}$.

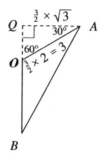

Then

$$\text{area of } \triangle OAB = \tfrac{1}{2}(\text{base} \times \text{height})$$

$$= \tfrac{1}{2}(3 \times \tfrac{3}{2}\sqrt{3})$$

$$= \tfrac{1}{2}(\tfrac{9}{2}\sqrt{3})$$

$$= \frac{9\sqrt{3}}{4}$$

CLIFFS QUICK REVIEW

Sentence Completion

1. (E) The missing word refers to something made up of *more than sixty citizens'groups,* so it must mean something like union or combination. The best choice is *coalition,* which means an alliance, especially a temporary one for some specific purpose, exactly the context here.

2. (D) The missing words must be in keeping with the phrase *a potent and hostile force.* Although choice (A) is not clearly wrong, it is not nearly as good a choice as *ruthless* and *brutal,* which directly describe something *hostile.*

3. (A) The sense of the sentence calls for words that say television includes stories of crimes but nearly eliminates other news. Either *reports* or *broadcasts* is a possible verb, and *exclusion, abandonment,* or *elimination* is a possible noun. Only choice (A) combines two of them.

4. (A) Since the *signs* are of *dangerous changes,* the missing adjective must be *ominous* (threatening, sinister).

5. (C) Since the results of the new bill are ironic, they will either benefit its opponents or harm its supporters. Of the five choices, only (C) clearly combines the *beneficiaries* (those who benefit) with the *adversaries* (those who oppose). Although *profiteers* and *freebooters* (plunderers) are both those who take advantage of something for their own gain, the words do not sensibly go with *of the new lower taxes.*

6. (C) Since the parallel adjective is *sympathetic* and the main clause describes a mistake, the missing adjective should have favorable connotations. Either (A) *affectionate* or (C) *discerning* is possible, but since the rest of the sentence describes what is clearly not *discerning* (perceptive) as opposed to what is *normally* the case, the better choice is (C). (Choice B, *forbearing,* means holding back and is neither favorable nor unfavorable.)

7. (E) From the context of the sentence, it is evident that the two blanks must be filled in with opposite words. Although choices (B), (D), and (E) each has a first word that would work, only (E) *disturbed . . nonchalantly* has a second word that would fit with *shrugged* (a shrug is a gesture that indicates unconcern).

8. (E) Although all of the adverbs might fit this sentence, both choice (A) and (C) do not quite fit the meaning of *can conceal its secrets almost permanently.* The only verb that makes complete sense in this context is *scrutinize* because the point of the sentence is that secret organizations cannot be closely watched and still be secret.

9. (B) Both of the adjectives must suggest solitude, but only in choice (B) are both words appropriate. *Private,* or *secluded,* or *claustrophobic* is suitable, but none of the others fits this context.

Analogies

10. (C) A *net* is the means by which one catches a *butterfly*; a *rabbit* may be caught in a *snare*. While you might pick up *dust* in a *dustpan* (B), you wouldn't catch it, so (B) is not the best choice.

11. (A) An *orb* is a sphere or globe, so the second of the two terms here defines the shape of the objects in the first. The best choice is *dice*, which are *cubes*. *Staircases*, choice (B), may be in the shape of *spirals*, but they are not necessarily so.

12. (E) A *calorie* is a unit of measurement that applies to *heat*. A *mile* is also a unit of measurement, one that applies to *distance*.

13. (D) If *oil* and *water* come in contact, the *oil* floats on top of the *water*. In the same way, a *boat* floats on top of a *lake*. You might be tempted to choose *milk* and *cream*, choice (D), because *cream* does float on *milk*. But the terms here are in the wrong order.

14. (D) To *ameliorate* is to make better, to improve; in this pairing, the action of the verb (*ameliorate*) brings about the noun (*improvement*). Choice (A) is close, but to *advertise* does not necessarily bring about a *sale*. Similarly, to *expedite* (the transitive verb meaning to hurry) does not necessarily result in *punctuality*. The best choice is *inoculate* (immunize), which brings about *immunity*.

15. (D) A great or large *fire* is called a *conflagration*. So the second word is the extreme of the first word. The extreme of *fear* is *terror*, so choice (D) is the best answer. Choice (A) *Armageddon*, is the extreme of *battle*, but the terms are in the wrong order. Choices (B), (C), and (E) give synonyms.

Critical Reading

16. (B) Choice (C) is incorrect; only one chapter of the book is devoted to women. Although the book was written to entertain the Duchess of Urbino, nothing implies that it is a collection of conversations *with* noblewomen, choice (D). Choices (A) and (E) are also clearly wrong; the book does not satirize nobles— on the contrary, it defines the ideal courtier—and although art, music, and poetry are mentioned as noble pursuits, they are not the main subject.

17. (D) Line 19 suggests that (D) is the best answer. Although a growing merchant class, choice (E), was interested in the ideas in the book, it was not chiefly responsible for spreading them. Choices (A), (B), and (C) have nothing to do with a wider audience for the book.

18. (C) Nothing in the passage suggests Castiglione's feelings about the structure of society. Choice (A) is indicated in lines 7-8, (B) in lines 2-4, (D) in lines 1-2, and (E) in lines 32-34.

19. (A) The context makes it clear that wealthy merchants could (and wanted to) copy the style of people who were part of Renaissance courts. They certainly wanted more than to praise or define it, choices (C) and (E), and they wouldn't aspire to refining it, choice (B). *Disparage,* choice (D), means to belittle, which is clearly incorrect.

20. (C) It is not implied that Sofonisba is boastful; nor is she a member of the merchant class, choice (B). She is also not set up as an ideal Renaissance woman, choice (D), or as a rebel, choice (A). Choice (E) is both irrelevant and wrong.

21. (E) Sofonisba and her sisters are used as examples of this point. Nothing suggests that the *quality* of women's education improved; lines 32-34 state that formal education for women remained poor. Choice (A) is irrelevant, and (B) is incorrect because Elisabetta Gonzaga was a member of a Renaissance court. Castiglione did not *urge* women to demand equality, choice (C); he defined the attributes of an ideal noblewoman.

22. (B) The author is presenting information in a straightforward way, neither moralizing, choice (A), nor arguing, choice (C). The tone is not somber (D), nor does the author make use of irony (E).

23. (C) Answer (C) is suggested by lines 2-4. Nothing in the passage suggests that hominids were mentally weaker than other savanna inhabitants, choice (A), or that their hunting skills were poorer than the carnivores', choice (D). It was their vulnerability, not their lack of skills, that presented a problem. Therefore, the author states that the hominids probably did not join the ranks of the carnivores, choice (B). Also, nothing indicates that hominids were the natural prey of other species, choice (E).

24. (A) The final paragraph theorizes that hominids branched into two populations, only one leading to *Homo sapiens,* choice (D). Choice (B) is vague, and (C) and (E) are both incorrect.

25. (E) The term *generalist* implies that hominids ate a variety of food. Since neither fruit nor nuts are meats, however, choice (A) is wrong. Choices (B), (C), and (D) are irrelevant.

26. (C) While choices (A), (D), and (E) were all problems, they result from, or are not as significant as, long dry periods. Choice (B) is incorrect; too much rainfall is never described as a problem.

27. (A) Lines 48-49 support choice (A) as the correct answer. The passage states that choices (B), (C), (D), and (E) all occur during dry periods.

28. (C) Although choices (A) and (E) are true, they are not the primary reasons the author describes conditions on the savanna. Choice (D) is incorrect; the Oklahoma land-rushers are used briefly as a contrast, not the other way around. Choice (B) is incorrect; this split isn't covered in the passage.

29. (D) Context makes it clear that choice (D) is the best answer. Lions and packs of hyenas are used by the author to illustrate why hominids didn't join the ranks of the carnivores. Therefore, choice (B) is incorrect. Only hyenas are described as traveling in packs, choice (A). Choices (C) and (E) are not supported by any information in the passage.

30. (E) It is the long dry periods that support the author's theory that some hominids were forced to use *their heads* to find food. Choice (A) would not change his theory but rather make the situation on the savanna more competitive. Choice (B) is irrelevant. The finding that fossil jaws varied in size, choice (C), would support the author's theory rather than call it into question, and (D) would not alter the problem of long periods of drought.

31. (C) The sentence doesn't prove anything, choice (A), nor is it ironic, choice (B). Choice (D) is not supported; the development of tools is not discussed in the passage. The term *outwitted* in choice (E) is not accurate; although humans' ancestors *used their heads* to find food, it is not implied that they tricked or outsmarted other species.

Quantitative Comparison

1. (C) Note that because 8 and 9 are present in both columns, you don't need to worry about them. Then in column A you have $7 + 10$ (which is 17), and in column B you have $6 + 11$ (which is also 17). So the two columns are equal.

2. (B) If $p - q < 0$, adding q to both sides, you get $p < q$. That is, column B is greater than column A.

3. (C) Suppose that you thought of 2. Doubling it gives you 4. Now also suppose that x is 3. Then adding 3 gives you 7. If you now divide by 2, you're left with 3.5. And if you now subtract the original number (2), you're left with $3.5 - 2 = 1.5$, which is half of x. Any number you try would give the same result. So column A is equal to column B.

4. (B) In a right triangle, the hypotenuse is the longest side. So in a triangle of sides 3", 4", and 5", the two perpendicular sides are 3" and 4".

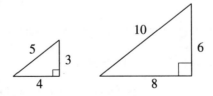

So

$$\text{area of triangle} = \tfrac{1}{2} \times \text{base} \times \text{height}$$
$$= \tfrac{1}{2} \times 4 \times 3$$
$$= 6 \text{ square inches}$$

And twice its area is 12 square inches.

In the right triangle of sides 6", 8", and 10", the two perpendicular sides are 6" and 8". So

$$\text{area of triangle} = \tfrac{1}{2} \times \text{base} \times \text{height}$$
$$= \tfrac{1}{2} \times 8 \times 6$$
$$= 24 \text{ square inches}$$

So column B is greater than column A.

5. (A) In any triangle, the longer side is opposite the larger angle.

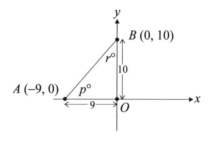

You can determine the longer side by the coordinates. In the given triangle, side OA is 9 units long and side OB is 10 units long. Because OB is longer than OA, angle p (which is opposite the longer side), is larger than angle r (which is opposite the shorter side). So $p > r$.

6. (A) The sum of all even integers between 2 and 10 inclusive can be written as

$$2 + 4 + 6 + 8 + 10$$

The sum of all odd integers between 1 and 11 inclusive can be written as

$$1 + 3 + 5 + 7 + 9 + 11$$

You can solve this problem by adding the two quantities. You might wish to quickly do the arithmetic mentally or by using your calculator.

$$2+4+6+8+10 = 30$$
$$1+3+5+7+9+11 = 36$$

Since $36 - 30 = 6$, column A is greater than column B.

7. (C) Because p, q, and r are consecutive negative integers, try some values, such as $p = -3$, $q = -2$, and $r = -1$. Then

$$\text{column A} = pr$$
$$= (-3)(-1)$$
$$= 3$$

and

$$\text{column B} = (q-1)(q+1)$$
$$= (-2-1)(-2+1)$$
$$= (-3)(-1)$$
$$= 3$$

So the two columns are equal.

Another way to solve this problem is to see that column A is the product of the least and the greatest of the three numbers. In column B, $q - 1$ is the least number (because q is the middle number and 1 less than it is going to be the least number), and $q + 1$ is the greatest number, which means that column B is also the product of the least and greatest of the three numbers.

8. (D) You know that s is less than 0, so try $s = -1$. And you know that t is greater than 0, so try $t = 2$. Then u is the average of s and t.

$$u = \frac{s + t}{2}$$
$$= \frac{-1 + 2}{2}$$
$$= \frac{1}{2}$$
$$= 0.5$$

So

$$\text{column A} = u = 0.5$$
$$\text{column B} = 0$$

In this case, column A is greater than column B.

What happens if $s = -1$ and $t = 1$?

$$u = \frac{s + t}{2}$$
$$= \frac{-1 + 1}{2}$$
$$= 0$$

So column A = 0, column B = 0, and column A equals column B.

As soon as you get two different comparisons (column A is greater in the first example, and the two columns are equal in the second), you know that the right answer has to be choice (D)—the relationship cannot be determined from the information given.

9. (B) An insightful method of solving this problem is as follows. Since John is traveling 30 miles per hour, in 1 hour he will travel 30 miles. Since Inga is traveling 60 miles per hour, in 1 hour she will travel 60 miles. So Inga will travel 30 miles farther in 1 hour. Because Inga is only 20 miles behind John, she will catch up to him in less than 1 hour.

Solving mathematically,

In the figure above, J is where John currently is, and I is where Inga currently is. When Inga catches up with John, she will have traveled x miles, and John will have traveled $x - 20$ miles. Assume that t is the amount of time (in hours) that passes before Inga catches up with John. So the distance traveled by Inga, x, is $60t$ (because distance equals rate times time). That is,

$$x = 60t$$

The distance traveled by John, $x - 20$, is $30t$. That is,

$$x - 20 = 30t$$

From the first equation you know that $x = 60t$. Substituting this value of x into the second equation, you get

$$60t - 20 = 30t$$
$$30t = 20$$
$$t = \tfrac{2}{3}$$

Since column B is 1 hour, it is greater than column A.

10. (A) To find p, note that EC is equal to x (because $AB=EC$). Then in $\triangle CDE$, all three sides are of the same length, x.

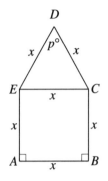

If the three sides of a triangle are equal, then each of the three angles of the triangle must be 60 degrees. That is, p must be 60, which means that column A is greater than column B.

11. (B) Notice that since there are values in each column, the answer cannot be (D). To actually make a comparison, first simplify column A.

$$\sqrt{.16} = .4$$

So you have $(.4)^{100}$ in column A.

Next simplify column B.

$$\sqrt{2} \cong 1.4$$

So you have $(1.4)^{10}$ in column B.

When you multiply a fraction times itself, it gets smaller, and when you multiply a mixed number times itself, it gets larger. Since column A started out smaller (.4) and will continue to get smaller, and since column B started out larger (1.4) and will continue to get larger, the correct answer is (B).

12. (B) Just to make things easier, assume that the cost of the sofa is $100. Then with a 10% discount, the cost is

$$100 - 10 = \$90$$

Add to it the 8% sales tax.

$$
\begin{aligned}
\text{price with tax} &= 90 + (.08 \times 90) \\
&= 90 + 7.20 \\
&= 97.20 \text{ (column A}
\end{aligned}
$$

If the sofa costs $100, column B is 98% of the cost (without the sales tax). So

$$
\begin{aligned}
\text{price without tax} &= .98 \times 100 \\
&= 98 \text{ (column B)}
\end{aligned}
$$

So column B is greater than column A.

Another method of solving the problem is to let x equal the cost of the sofa.

$$
\begin{aligned}
\text{column A} &= (.90x)(1.08) \\
&= .972x \\
\text{column B} &= .98x
\end{aligned}
$$

13. (D) Although the figure is not drawn to scale, the information tells you that angle w is greater than angle z (because in a triangle, an angle across from a longer side is a greater angle).

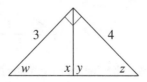

In the drawing, angles x and y may appear to be equal. If they are, then angle w plus angle x would be greater than angle y

plus angle *z*. However, you can't be sure that angle *x* and angle *y* are equal. They could, for example, vary as shown below.

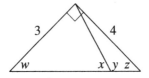

In this variation of the figure, by observation, angles *w* and *x* total less than do angles *y* and *z*. Since column A could be greater or less than column B, no comparison can be made and (D) is the correct answer.

14. (A) You know that the total surface area of a cube is

$$\text{total surface area} = 6 \times \text{surface area of one surface}$$

$$54 = 6 \times \text{surface area of one surface}$$

$$54 \div 6 = \text{surface area of one surface}$$

$$9 = \text{surface area of one surface}$$

The surface area of any one surface is the square of one edge of the cube (because in a cube all edges are of the same length). So

$9 = $ square of one edge

$3 = $ length of each edge

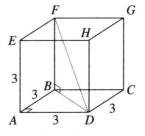

In the diagram above, the distance from one of the top corners (for example, point *F*) to a bottom corner on the opposite side (for example, point *D*) is the longest diagonal. Some other such equal diagonals are *HB, EC,* and *AG*. If *FD* is the longest diagonal, you can find its length by first finding the length of *BD*.

Note that *ABCD* is a square of side 3. So in $\triangle ABD$, $AD = 3$, $AB = 3$, and *AD* is perpendicular to *AB*. Then

$$c^2 = a^2 + b^2$$
$$(BD)^2 = (AB)^2 + (AD)^2$$
$$= 3^2 + 3^2$$
$$= 18$$
$$BD = \sqrt{18}, \text{ or approximately } 4.2$$

Since *FD* is even longer than *BD,* column A is greater than column B.

To complete the problem mathematically, you would proceed as follows. Notice also that *FB* and *BD* are perpendicular to each other. Then

$$c^2 = a^2 + b^2$$
$$(FD)^2 = (FB)^2 + BD^2$$
$$= 3^2 + 18 \text{ (from above)}$$
$$= 9 + 18$$
$$= 27$$
$$FD = \sqrt{27}$$
$$= \sqrt{9 \times 3}$$
$$= 3\sqrt{3}$$

So column A is $3\sqrt{3}$ and column B is 4. Because $\sqrt{3}$ is greater than 1.5, 3 times $\sqrt{3}$ will be greater than 4. (Another way of comparing $3\sqrt{3}$ and 4 is to see that the square of $3\sqrt{3}$ is 27, which you found above, and the square of 4 is 16, which means that $3\sqrt{3}$ is greater than 4.)

15. (A) First find the area of $\triangle ABC$. If you take AC as the base, which is 30, and BD as the height, which is 13, the area of the triangle is

$$\tfrac{1}{2} \times \text{base} \times \text{height} = \tfrac{1}{2} \times 30 \times 13$$
$$= 195$$

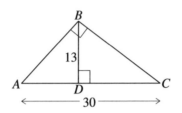

To find the area of the triangle, you can also consider AB as the base and BC as the height, as these two sides are perpendicular to each other. Then the area of the triangle is

$$\tfrac{1}{2} \times \text{base} \times \text{height} = \tfrac{1}{2} \times AB \times BC$$

Because the area, as you found previously, is 195, you can write

$$195 = \tfrac{1}{2} \times AB \times BC$$
$$390 = AB \times BC = (\text{column A})$$

So column A (390) is greater than column B (360).

Grid-In Questions

16. (45) To solve this problem, you need to remember that opposite angles (vertical angles) are always equal. With this information, you can fill out the angular measures as shown in the following diagram.

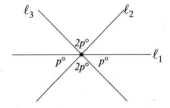

Consider the angles about the point marked on ℓ_1. The angular measure of a straight line is 180°. Then,

$$p + 2p + p = 180$$
$$4p = 180$$
$$p = 45$$

17. (30) The perimeter of a square is four times the length of one side. So

$$100 = 4(q - 5)$$
$$100 = 4q - 20$$
$$100 + 20 = 4q$$
$$120 = 4q$$
$$\frac{120}{4} = q$$
$$30 = q$$

18. $\left(\frac{20}{6} \text{ or } \frac{10}{3} \text{ or } 3.33\right)$ Notice that there are six spaces between 0 and 5. So each space has a value of $\frac{5}{6}$. Point T is four spaces from 0, so

$$T = 4 \times \frac{5}{6}$$
$$= \frac{20}{6}$$
$$= \frac{10}{3}$$
$$\cong 3.33$$

19. (80) In $\triangle CDE$, because $\angle E$ is 80°, the other two angles must add up to 100°. That is, $x + y = 100$.

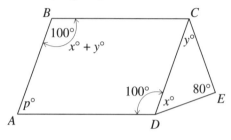

In a parallelogram, the diagonally opposite angles are equal and the four angles add up to 360°. You know that $x + y = 100$, which means that $\angle B$ is 100° and so $\angle D$ must also be 100°. Together these two angles add up to 200°. The remaining two angles, $\angle A$ and $\angle C$, must add up to $360 - 200 = 160°$. Because $\angle A = \angle C$, each angle must be 80°.

20. (99) Assume that the company's first-year earnings were $100. Then its second-year earnings were 10% more, which is

$$100 + 10 = 110$$

The company's third-year earnings were 10% less than its second-year earnings, which is

$$110 - (10\% \text{ of } 110) = 110 - 11$$
$$= 99$$

So, as a percent, the company's third-year earnings compared to its first-year earnings were

$$\tfrac{99}{100} \times 100 = 99$$

21. (2,340) The first slot has 26 possibilities (because there are 26 letters in the alphabet). The second slot has 10 possibilities (from 0 to 9 inclusive). The third slot has 9 possibilities (because one of the numeric digits is used in the second slot, and it cannot be repeated).

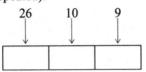

So

$$\text{total number of possibilities} = 26 \times 10 \times 9$$
$$= 2{,}340$$

22. (16)

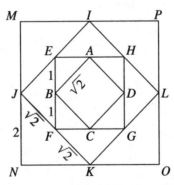

Side AB is the hypotenuse of $\triangle AEB$. Also, $EB = EA$. So

$$c^2 = a^2 + b^2$$
$$\left(\sqrt{2}\right)^2 = (EB)^2 + (EA)^2$$
$$2 = (EB)^2 + (EA)^2$$
$$2 = 2(EB)^2 \qquad \text{(because } EB = EA\text{)}$$
$$1 = EB$$

If $EB = 1$, then $EF = 2$. And EF is the hypotenuse of $\triangle EJF$. Then

$$c^2 = a^2 + b^2$$
$$(EF)^2 = (FJ)^2 + (JE)^2$$
$$2^2 = 2(FJ)^2 \qquad \text{(because } FJ = JE)$$
$$4 = 2(FJ)^2$$
$$2 = (FJ)^2$$
$$\sqrt{2} = FJ$$

If $FJ = \sqrt{2}$, then $JK = 2\sqrt{2}$. And JK is the hypotenuse of $\triangle JNK$. Then

$$c^2 = a^2 + b^2$$
$$(JK)^2 = (JN)^2 + (NK)^2$$
$$\left(2\sqrt{2}\right)^2 = 2(JN)^2 \qquad \text{(because } JN = NK)$$
$$4(2) = 2(JN)^2$$
$$8 = 2(JN)^2$$
$$4 = (JN)^2$$
$$2 = JN$$

If $JN = 2$, then $MN = 2(JN) = 4$. Because $MNOP$ is a square,
$$\text{area} = 4 \times 4$$
$$= 16$$

23. (8) The value of $7*$ is $7 + 8 = 15$.

The value of $9*$ is $9 - 8 = 1$.

Then the value of $(7* + 9*)$ is $15 + 1 = 16$.

And the value of $(7* + 9*)*$ is $16* = 16 - 8 = 8$.

24. (4) You know that the total is 30. So you can write

$$30 = 7 + 8 + t + 6 + u$$
$$30 = 21 + t + u$$
$$9 = t + u$$

To find the median, you should first arrange the numbers in an increasing (or decreasing) order because the median is the number in the middle. A partial order of the numbers is

6, 7, 8

You need to place t and u in the set above. You know that the median is 6, which means that 6 should be the number in the middle and which further means that both t and u should be to the left of 6 (that is, less than 6). You also know that u is greater than t. Then the set of numbers is

$t, u,$ 6, 7, 8

The sum of t and u must be 9 (because 6, 7, and 8 sum to 21, and the total, 30, less 21 is 9). So the only possible values for t and u are 4 and 5, respectively. So $t = 4$.

25. (4) Triangle *DBC* is a $30°-60°-90$ triangle, which means that sides *DB, BC,* and *CD* are in the ratio $1:\sqrt{2}:2,$ respectively.

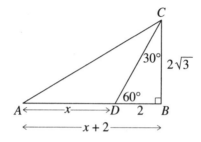

You're given that *BC* is $2\sqrt{3}$, which means that the common factor for all three sides is 2. Then side *BD* is $2 \times 1 = 2$. If *BD* $= 2$, then *AB* $= x + 2$. The area of $\triangle ABC$ is given as $6\sqrt{3}$. So

$$\text{area} = \tfrac{1}{2} \times \text{base} \times \text{height}$$

$$6\sqrt{3} = \tfrac{1}{2}(AB)(BC)$$

$$6\sqrt{3} = \tfrac{1}{2}(x+2)\left(2\sqrt{3}\right)$$

$$6\sqrt{3} = \frac{(x+2)\left(\cancel{2}\sqrt{3}\right)}{\cancel{2}}$$

$$6\sqrt{3} = (x+2)\sqrt{3}$$

$$6 = x + 2$$

$$6 - 2 = x$$

$$4 = x$$

Sentence Completion

1. (C) The missing word must mean large, since the lobby holds many chairs without crowding. Of the five choices, only *spacious,* which means vast or extensive, is suitable.

2. (B) The logic of the sentence calls for an adjective and a verb that are both positive or both negative. In choices (C), (D), and (E), one of the two words is positive and one negative. Only choice (B) has an adjective that means skilled and a verb that means to be superior.

3. (C) The best choice in this context is *antidote,* which means a remedy to counteract an evil.

4. (A) If the missing noun suggests a decline, the missing verb must be positive, and vice versa. Choices (C), (D), and (E) suggest a rise or a stability in the currency, but the verbs are positive. Both choice (A) and choice (B) have nouns that denote a fall in value, but only (A) has the logical verb *effected* (brought about).

5. (D) The missing noun must describe something even worse than a *heavy defeat.* The best choice is *debacle,* a rout or great disaster.

6. (E) Both of the missing terms must describe programs that are not *efficient and streamlined* and that appear to have *happened spontaneously.* The words *sophisticated, refined, smooth,* and *methodical* are inappropriate, so only choice (E), which uses *rudimentary* (elementary, imperfectly developed) and *improvisational,* fits.

7. (B) Of the five choices, only (B) *preservation* fits the context of the sentence and makes sense. *Cold, dark, airless waters* might help preserve something. They would not *restore* (A) or *renovate* (E) something.

8. (D) Since the book was eventually published to become *famous,* you can eliminate choice (A) *definitively* (finally) and choice (B) *ultimately.* Since the comment is not perceptive, you can eliminate (C) *insightful,* and since it isn't wordy, you can eliminate (E) *verbose.* The book was turned down at first (*initially*) with a comment that is concerned with how well it might sell in the United States (*commercial*).

9. (B) Since the sentence refers to *divergent strong opinions,* the two words should be both opposites and forceful. Choices (A) and (E) are strong, but both are negative, while both the nouns in choice (D) are favorable. *Indifference* in (C) is not a strong opinion. The correct choice is (B): *praise* and *vilification* (strong disapproval).

10. (E) Choices (A), (C), (D), and (E) are all possible fill-ins for the first blank, but choice (E) *innate* (inborn, natural) is the best choice for the second blank.

Analogies

11. (B) A *tablespoon* and a *cup* are specific units of measurement in cooking, and there are sixteen *tablespoon*s in a *cup. Ounce* and *pint* are also units of measurements, and there are sixteen *ounce*s in a *pint.*

12. (E) The first of the two nouns, *caffeine,* is a stimulant that may interfere with or have an effect on *sleep.* Of the five choices, the closest is *smog,* which may interfere with or affect *respiration.*

13. (B) A *lyric* is a short poem or the text, as opposed to the music, of a song. It is composed of *words*. Similarly, a *song* is composed of *notes*.

14. (E) A *comedy,* a comic play, is performed before an audience in a *theater,* as a *game,* also a form of entertainment, is performed in a *stadium*. A *film* might be performed (shown) at a *festival,* but since a *theater* and a *stadium* are physical structures and a *festival* is not, (E) is the best choice.

15. (C) A *broker* is one who sells stocks, and her or his office or place of business is a *brokerage*. The worker-to-place-of-work connection is repeated in *astronomer* and *observatory*.

16. (D) To *guffaw* is to *laugh* in a loud or coarse manner. The closest analogy is to *gobble,* to *eat* quickly and greedily. The *sip : drink* analogy is close, but there is no connotation of coarseness in the verb *drink*.

17. (B) A *levee* is an embankment by a river built to prevent a *flood*. The relationship here is that the first term is intended to prevent or guard against the second. A *dam* may control the flow of a *river,* but it is not intended to prevent a river. The purpose of a *vaccine,* however, is to guard against a disease, such as *polio*.

18. (A) A *despairing* person has no *hope* as an *indigent* person has no *money*. Although an *angry* person may sometimes lose *control,* lack of *control* is not a definition of the adjective *angry* as lack of *hope* defines *despairing*.

19. (B) The verb describes the function or purpose of the noun; an *alarm* is intended to *warn*. Although most of the verbs describe an action associated with the noun, this action is not the purpose of the noun. An *ambulance* may use or need to *speed,* but this is not its purpose. The best choice is *yeast,* the purpose of which is to *leaven,* to produce fermentation in dough.

20. (A) *Magma* is molten rock. The liquid-to-solid relationship is analogous to the relationship of *water* to *ice*.

21. (C) A *palindrome* is a word or sentence that reads the same backward and forward, such as *radar* or *level* or *Able was I ere I saw Elba*. In this pairing, the second word is an example of the first. *Onomatopoeia* is a word formed to imitate the sound that it denotes, such as *buzz* or *bang*.

22. (E) *Inveterate* and *superficial* are adjectives with opposite meanings. *Inveterate* means deep-rooted, while *superficial* means of the surface, shallow. Of the five choices, the only pair of opposites is *conspicuous* (easily seen) and *imperceptible* (difficult to perceive).

23. (C) *Archaic* and *antiquated* are synonyms. They both mean ancient. Choice (C) *prodigal* (recklessly extravagant) and *wasteful* are the only pair of synonyms of the choices given.

Critical Reading

24. (B) Lines 16-18 suggest that choice (B) is the best answer. Although many in England may have agreed with choices (A), (D), and (E), these points are not mentioned as respresenting the position of British constitutional theorists. Choice (C) is simply incorrect.

25. (A) The passage does not mention choices (B), (C), (D), or (E), but the effect of the colonists' location and tradition of managing their own affairs is implied (lines 26-32).

26. (D) In context, *consent* is the equivalent of parliamentary *representation*. Choices (A) and (E), although desired by the colonists, are not equivalent to the concept of consent, and (B) is inadequate; the colonists desired more than consideration. Choice (C) is irrelevant and incorrect.

27. (B) The implication is that members of Parliament were responsive to their own class and those who elected them, not to everyone—for example, the poor. Nothing in the passage implies that Parliament *opposed* inequality (A) or that the members of Parliament received bribes (D). Choice (C) is also irrelevant, and (E) is simply incorrect.

28. (C) Lines 32-34 make it clear that the Stamp Act made armed conflict inevitable, and from the rest of the passage it is clear that the primary issue was taxation. The mail system was not an issue (don't be misled by *stamp*). Also, the right to free speech isn't addressed in the passage. Although many in Parliament felt the colonists' demands were treasonable, nothing suggests that the Stamp Act was used as a punishment. Choice (E) is irrelevant.

29. (D) The Revenue Act was designed to raise money for the British treasury. All the other choices are cited as sources of justification of or support for the colonists.

30. (C) Lines 41-51 suggest that (C) is the best answer. Otis's tracts (B) were a result of the shift, not a cause. Choice (D) is incorrect; the colonists were not impressed by the examples of Manchester and Birmingham. While choices (A) and (E) may be true, they are not cited as the reasons the colonists changed the basis of their claims.

31. (D) See lines 65-66. Choice (B) is incorrect; Otis stated that property alone was not the basis of government (lines 66-68). A true government, not property or constitutions (E), has its *everlasting foundation* in God and the *necessities of our nature* (lines 86-88). Choice (A) is not stated or implied by Otis.

32. (C) While Otis might agree with choices (A), (B), and even (E), they are not statements of the main idea in his tract. Otis would not agree with choice (D) (lines 87-88).

33. (A) In context, (A) is the best choice. Choice (B) is the opposite of the intended meaning; Otis sees the laws of nature as part of God's design. Complexity (C) is not suggested by context. Although *mechanically* might in some instances suggest artificiality (D), this is not true here—Otis focuses on the naturalness of these occurrences (notice the word preceding *mechanically*). Efficiency (E) might be a result of the mechanical operation of the laws of nature, but this is not the best definition.

34. (C) See the last paragraph. Choices (A) and (E) are vague; also, Otis does not describe the universe as unpredictable. Otis doesn't address a person's proper station (B), and *God* or *Nature* is not synonymous with *Church* (D).

35. (C) Choices (A) and (D) are secondary to the main purpose. Choice (B) is vague; also, *cruelty* doesn't describe Parliament's position, nor are any treasonable *acts* of colonists described. Choice (E) is incorrect; two taxation acts are mentioned, but these references don't constitute tracing the history.

1. (B) If

$$\frac{5}{a+b} = 25$$

which is the same as

$$\frac{5}{a+b} = \frac{25}{1}$$

then by cross-multiplying you get

$$5 = 25(a+b)$$

Dividing both sides by 25, you get

$$\frac{5}{25} = \frac{25(a+b)}{25}$$

Canceling,

$$\frac{\cancel{5}^{\,1}}{\cancel{25}\,5} = \frac{\cancel{25}(a+b)}{\cancel{25}}$$

So

$$\tfrac{1}{5} = a+b$$

2. (B) You know that $k + m = n + p$ and that $m = n + 1$. Substitute the value of $m = (n+1)$ in the first equation. Then

$$k + (n+1) = n + p$$
$$k + n + 1 - n = p$$
$$k + 1 = p$$
$$k = p - 1$$

3. (C) You know that $\angle POQ$ is 120°. That is,

$$r + s + t + u = 120$$

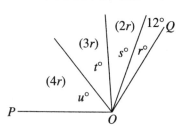

Substituting the value of s, t, and u, you get

$$r + 2r + 3r + 4r = 120$$
$$10r = 120$$
$$r = 12$$

You know that $t = 3r$. So $t = 3 \times 12 = 36$.

4. (B) As shown in the figure below, Brigitte's trip from her home to Addison and then to Belville forms a right angle. The return trip from Belville then is the hypotenuse of a right triangle.

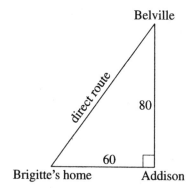

Using the Pythagorean theorem, you can write

$$c^2 = a^2 + b^2$$
$$(\text{direct route})^2 = 60^2 + 80^2$$
$$= 3,600 + 6,400$$
$$= 10,000$$
$$\text{direct route} = \sqrt{10,000}$$
$$= 100$$

The distance from Brigitte's home to Belville via Addison is

$$60 + 80 = 140$$

So the direct route is shorter by $140 - 100 = 40$ miles. You may have been able to quickly figure out the direct route if you noticed the $3 : 4 : 5$ ratio of the sides (6, 8, 10; 60, 80, 100).

5. (A)

From 1970 to 1975, the increase was $400 - 320 = 80$.

From 1975 to 1980, the increase was $450 - 400 = 50$.

From 1980 to 1985, the increase was $450 - 450 = 0$.

From 1985 to 1990, the increase was $360 - 450 = -90$.

From 1990 to 1995, the increase was $400 - 360 = 40$.

So the greatest increase was from 1970 to 1975.

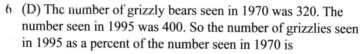

6. (D) The number of grizzly bears seen in 1970 was 320. The number seen in 1995 was 400. So the number of grizzlies seen in 1995 as a percent of the number seen in 1970 is

$$\frac{\text{number seen in 1995}}{\text{number seen in 1970}} \times 100 = \frac{400}{320} \times 100$$

$$= \frac{40}{32} \times 100$$

$$= \frac{5}{4} \times 100$$

$$= 125$$

So the percent is 125.

7. (D) The best way to solve this problem is to plug in the answer choices. You're looking for a value of $2p + 4$ that is *not* divisible by 9.

Choice (A): If $p = -11$,

$$2p + 4 = 2(-11) + 4$$

$$= -22 + 4$$

$$= -18$$

This *is* divisible by 9.

Choice (B): If $p = 2.5$,

$$2p + 4 = 2(2.5) + 4$$

$$= 5 + 4$$

$$= 9$$

This *is* divisible by 9.

Choice (C): If $p = 7$,

$$2p + 4 = 2(7) + 4$$

$$= 14 + 4$$

$$= 18$$

This *is* divisible by 9.

Choice (D): If $p = 9$,

$$2p + 4 = 2(9) + 4$$
$$= 18 + 4$$
$$= 22$$

This is *not* divisible by 9. So it has to be the right answer. At this point, you can stop because you've found the correct choice.

8. (C) The slope of the line is 1, which means that for every change of 1 unit along the y-axis, there is a change of 1 unit along the x-axis. Or, for a change of -1 along the y-axis, the corresponding change along the x-axis is also -1. If you constructed a line from the origin points $(0, 0)$, each choice would have the following slopes:

Choice (A), $(3, 1)$: change of 1 along the y-axis; change of 3 along the x-axis.

Choice (B), $(-3, 1)$: change of 1 along the y-axis; change of -3 along the x-axis.

Choice (C), $(-1,-1)$: change of -1 along the y-axis; change of -1 along the x-axis. *This is the correct slope. So it is the right answer.*

Choice (D), $(1, 3)$: change of 3 along the y-axis; change of 1 along the x-axis.

Choice (E), $(-1, 3)$: change of 3 along the y-axis; change of -1 along the x-axis.

9. (C) $p + 3q + 4r - 5s = 10$ You're given

and $\quad 3p + 9q = 12$

If you divide the second equation by 3, you get

$$\frac{\cancel{3}p + \cancel{9}^3 q}{\cancel{3}} = \frac{\cancel{12}^4}{\cancel{3}}$$

$$p + 3q = 4$$

Now substitute this value of $p + 3q$ in the first equation. So

$$p + 3q + 4r - 5s = 10$$

becomes

$$4 + 4r - 5s = 10$$
$$4r - 5s = 10 - 4$$
$$4r - 5s = 6$$

If you multiply both sides by 2, you get

$$2(4r - 5s) = 2(6)$$
$$8r - 10s = 12$$

10. (D) The area of a parallelogram is base × height.

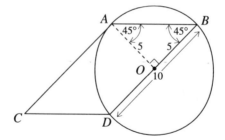

You can take side *DB* as the base. Since *DB* is the diameter of the circle with radius 5, $DB = 10$. To find the height, connect O to *A*. In $\triangle OAB, OA = OB = 5$, since each is the radius of the circle. Because $OA = OB$, $\angle OAB = \angle OBA = 45°$. Therefore, in $\triangle OAB$, two angles are 45° each, which means that

$$\angle BOA = 180 - 45 - 45 = 90°$$

If *DB* is the base of the parallelogram and $\angle BOA$ is 90°, you can take *OA* to be the height of the parallelogram. Since *OA* is 5,

$$\text{area of parallelogram} = \text{base} \times \text{height}$$
$$= 10 \times 5$$
$$= 50$$

CLIFFS QUICK REVIEW

1. (C) The first incident shows Douglass handling the issue of separate seating, and the second shows a white man doing the same. Although the first incident illustrates Douglass's wit, the second does not, choice (A). Kindness is not illustrated in the first incident, choice (B). Choices (D) and (E) are incorrect; (D) is irrelevant, and bitterness of whites (E) is not shown in the incidents.

2. (E) *Loafers* suggests that the people spent much of their time hanging out in the bar. Douglass is not generalizing about whites, however, choice (A). Choice (B) is unsupported by information in the passage. Choices (C) and (D) may be true, but there is no evidence to support either statement.

3. (C) Lines 17-22 support choice (C) as the best answer. When Douglass decides to wait for the second table, it is out of prudence (line 21), not out of a desire to make a statement, choice (B), or serve as a role model, choice (E). He doesn't know with whom he will be sitting, and therefore choice (A) is incorrect. Also, when he chooses the second table, he does not know he will provoke a dispute with the steward, choice (D).

4. (D) Douglass was not opposed to physical combat, as shown by his willingness to fight the steward if necessary (lines 29-32). Choice (A) is implied by the fact that the gentleman at the table knew Douglass by name (lines 41-42); choice (B) is implied by Douglass's desire not to sit with the *rough element,* by his diction, and by his reaction to the gentleman at the table; choice (C) is implied in lines 29-32. Douglass's sense of humor, choice (E), is shown in the way he handles the first incident described in the passage.

5. (A) It is ironic that animals are more civilized than people. Choice (D) is the second best answer, although it isn't clear that Douglass is using the term *sable brethren* ironically. Choices (A), (C), and (E) are not ironic.

6. (D) The primary contrast in the passage is between whites and African-Americans. On the basis of their comments to Du Bois (lines 50-52), these whites are obviously Northerners, not Southerners, choice (C). Although Europe is mentioned as being different from America in its treatment of African-Americans, this contrast isn't elaborated upon, choice (A). There is no support for either choice (B) or choice (E).

7. (C) Lines 52-55 suggest that (C) is the best choice (. . . *I smile, or am interested, or reduce the boiling to simmer* but *To the real question . . . I answer seldom a word*). These responses are clearly not angry, argumentative, or cruel, choices (A) and (D). Whereas Du Bois might be learned and philosophical in his writing, his description of these responses shows that they are not, choice (B). Also, he is perhaps misleading, but he is polite, not mocking, choice (E).

8. (D) The experience of being a problem is *peculiar, even for one who has never been anything else;* therefore, white people would have no chance of understanding an answer. The passage doesn't suggest that these people would ignore him (A), betray him (B), or persecute him (C). Perhaps the question itself can be seen as a sign of prejudice, choice (E), but Du Bois doesn't indicate that he sees it that way.

9. (A) *With a glance* suggests that the girl didn't think twice. The other definitions of *peremptorily* are incorrect, although one or more of them might describe what was in the girl's mind.

10. (B) See lines 69-70. Du Bois does not feel contempt for himself, choice (A), as is shown by his willingness to compete. Although one might expect the reactions in choices (C), (D), and (E), they are not Du Bois's, according to the passage. Choose your answer based on the passage, not on what one might expect.

11. (D) See lines 71-76. Du Bois wants the prizes; he doesn't despise them, choice (A). There is no evidence that his motives are altruistic, choice (B), or that he is more intelligent than the others, choice (C). Although he wants to *wrest* the prizes from the whites, he is not bent on revenge, choice (E).

12. (B) His *fiercely sunny* strife is contrasted to the hate-filled strife of other *black boys,* choice (A); he is ambitious and confident. Although the description might be seen as paradoxical, it is not mocking (E) or ironic (C), nor does it ridicule (D) other African-Americans, for whom he feels compassion.

13. (C) The prison-house has walls *strait and stubborn* that close around *everyone,* not just African-Americans, choice (A). The image clearly refers to life beyond school, choice (B), and while choices (D) and (E) may be the results of living in the prison-house, they are not themselves the prison.

14. (D) Choice (A) applies only to Passage 2. Choices (B) and (C) don't apply to both passages and in fact aren't supported by either. Neither passage advocates civil disobedience, choice (E).

15. (B) Avoid answer choices that use words such as *none, never,* and *always.* Although Passage 2 uses *more* rhetorical devices (such as figures of speech), Passage 1 uses some, for example, *his eyes were full of fire. I saw the lightning flash, but I could not tell where it would strike* and *voice . . . resounded like a clap of summer thunder.* All of the other answers correctly contrast the two passages.

1. (E) Since $(p - q) = 2^2$ is given, you know that $(p - q) = 4$. Then

$$[2(p-q)]^2 = [2(4)]^2$$
$$= 8^2$$
$$= 64$$

2. (D) You know that Raul spent one third of his pocket money on a video game. That means he still had two thirds of his pocket money left. Also, you know that this two thirds is equal to $6. If two thirds is $6, the one third he spent on the game is $3, and $6 + $3 = $9. Working it out another way,

$$\frac{2}{3} \text{ of the pocket money} = 6$$

$$\frac{2x}{3} = 6$$

Multiply each side by $\frac{3}{2}$.

$$\left(\frac{3}{2}\right)\frac{2x}{3} = \frac{6}{1}^3\left(\frac{3}{2}\right)$$
$$x = 3(3)$$
$$x = 9$$

That is, the total amount of his pocket money was $9.

3 (A) You know that

$$\frac{d}{c} = \frac{4}{3}$$

This equation can also be written as

$$\frac{c}{d} = \frac{3}{4}$$

If

$$\frac{a}{b} = \frac{c}{d}$$

Then

$$\frac{c}{d} = \frac{3}{4}$$

$$\frac{a}{b} = \frac{3}{4}$$

$$\left(\frac{a}{b}\right)^2 = \left(\frac{3}{4}\right)^2$$

$$= \frac{3}{4}\left(\frac{3}{4}\right) = \frac{9}{16}$$

4. (E) If 3 is the product of $\frac{1}{3}$ and x, you can write

$$3 = \tfrac{1}{3}(x)$$

Multiplying both sides by 3, you get

$$9 = x$$

If x is 9, then the sum of $\frac{1}{3}$ and x is $9\frac{1}{3}$.

5. (D) If 30 is 15% of x, you can write

$$15\% \text{ of } x = 30$$

$$.15x = 30$$

Dividing each side by .15 gives

$$\frac{.15x}{.15} = \frac{30}{.15}$$
$$x = 200$$

You could also solve this problem by working from the answer choices.

6. (B) Let B be Barry's current age and A be Al's current age. Then, because Barry is 20 years older than Al, you can write

$$B = A + 20$$

In 10 years, Barry and Al will both have aged by 10 years, so their ages will be $B + 10$ and $A + 10$, respectively. You know from the second part of the problem that, after 10 years, Barry's age will be twice Al's age. That is,

$$B + 10 = 2(A + 10)$$
$$B + 10 = 2A + 20$$
$$B = 2A + 20 - 10$$
$$B = 2A + 10$$

Substituting this value of B in the first equation, you get

$$B = A + 20$$
$$2A + 10 = A + 20$$

Subtracting 10 from each side leaves

$$2A = A + 10$$

Then subtracting A from each side leaves

$$A = 10$$

That is, Al's current age is 10. Since Al is 10 and Barry is 20 years older, Barry's current age is 30.

7. (B) If there are 5,280 feet in 1 mile,

$$\frac{1}{2} \text{ mile} = \frac{5,280}{2}$$
$$= 2,640 \text{ feet}$$

When the tape measure reads 1 foot, the correct length is 1 inch short of that. Then when the tape measure reads 2,640 feet (half a mile), the correct length will be short of that by 2,640 inches, and

$$\frac{2,640}{12} = 220 \text{ feet}$$

Therefore, the correct length is $\frac{1}{2}$ mile $- 220$ feet.

8. (A) The best way to solve this problem is to draw a diagram.

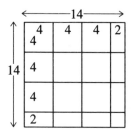

In the diagram shown above, when 9 squares, each of side 4, are cut from the sheet of paper, there is a 2-inch strip left along two sides of the paper that cannot be used. So the maximum number of squares that can be cut is 9.

9. (A) You're given
$$7x + 14y = 35$$

Dividing each side by 7, you get
$$x + 2y = 5$$

Multiplying both sides by 2, you get
$$2x + 4y = 10$$

10. (C) If the width of the rectangle is w, its length is $1.5w$.

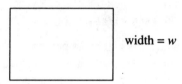

length = $1.5w$

width = w

Then
$$\text{perimeter} = 2(\text{length} \times \text{width})$$
$$20 = 2(1.5w + w)$$
$$20 = 2(2.5w)$$
$$20 = 5w$$
$$\frac{\cancel{20}^{\,4}}{\cancel{5}} = \frac{\cancel{5}w}{\cancel{5}}$$
$$4 = w$$

If the width is 4, then the length is $1.5 \times 4 = 6$, and the area is $4 \times 6 = 24$.

11. (E) Each employee who works 20 hours per week earns $300. So the total earned by these 20 employees is

$$300 \times 20 = \$6,000$$

Each employee who works 30 hours per week earns $400. So the total earned by these 5 employees is

$$400 \times 5 = \$2,000$$

Each employee who works 40 hours per week earns $800. So the total earned by these 5 employees is

$$800 \times 5 = \$4,000$$

So the total amount earned by 30 employees is

$$6,000 + 2,000 + 4,000 = \$12,000$$

12. (A) A person who works 40 hours per week earns $800. A person who works 10 hours per week earns $200. So as a percent, the earnings of a person who works 40 hours per week compared to the earnings of a person who works 10 hours per week is

$$\frac{800}{200} \times 100 = \frac{8}{2} \times 100$$
$$= 4 \times 100$$
$$= 400$$

13. (B) If PQ is the diameter, OQ is the radius (as is OP).

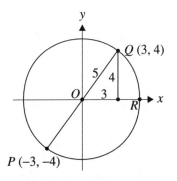

The length of the radius (as shown in the figure above) can be found by using the Pythagorean theorem.

$$c^2 = a^2 + b^2$$

$$(OQ)^2 = 3^2 + 4^2$$

$$(OQ)^2 = 9 + 16$$

$$(OQ)^2 = 25$$

$$OQ = \sqrt{25}$$

$$OQ = 5$$

(If you notice that this is a 3-4-5 right triangle, you wouldn't need to work out the Pythagorean theorem.)

If the radius of the circle is 5, then OR must also be 5, which means that the coordinates of R must be (5, 0). So this point lies on the circle.

14. (B) The length of the semicircle = 60π inches.

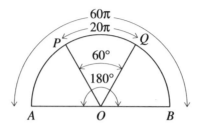

Remember that a semicircle measures 180°. Since $\angle POQ$ is 60°, then arc PQ also measures 60° (the central angle has the same degree measure as the arc it connects to). Since 60 is one third of 180, arc PQ is one third of the semicircle. Therefore, arc PQ must also be one third of 60π inches, which is 20π inches.

15. (D) You can solve this problem by plugging in the answer choices. You should start with choice (C) 3, which is the number of dimes. If she has 3 dimes and 7 pennies, she has 10 coins. You know she has a total of 14 coins, which means she must have 4 nickels. Then the total amount of money would be

$$7 \text{ pennies} = 7 \text{ cents}$$
$$3 \text{ dimes} = 30 \text{ cents}$$
$$4 \text{ nickels} = 20 \text{ cents}$$
$$\text{Total: } 14 \text{ coins} = 57 \text{ cents}$$

This is too low because you know that she has 62 cents. If choice (C) is too low, then choices (A) and (B) must also be too low. At this point, you can knock out choices (A), (B), and (C).

Now try choice (D) 4. If she has 4 dimes and 7 pennies, she has 11 coins, which means she must have 3 nickels. Then the total amount of money would be

$$7 \text{ pennies} = 7 \text{ cents}$$
$$4 \text{ dimes} = 40 \text{ cents}$$
$$3 \text{ nickels} = 15 \text{ cents}$$
$$\text{Total: } 14 \text{ coins} = 62 \text{ cents}$$

Choice (D) 4 works, so it has to be the right answer.

16. **(C)** After the first mile, each additional half mile is $0.40, which means that each additional mile is
$$2 \times 0.40 = \$0.80$$

For the 6-mile trip, the cost is $2.00 for the first mile plus the cost for 5 additional miles. Because each additional 1 mile costs $0.80, the cost for 5 additional miles is
$$0.80 \times 5 = \$4.00$$

Therefore, the total cost for the 6-mile trip is
$$2.00 + 4.00 = \$6.$$

For the 3-mile trip, the cost is $2.00 for the first mile plus the cost for 2 additional miles ($1.60) for a total of $3.60.

Therefore, the ratio of the two amounts is
$$\frac{6.00}{3.60} = \frac{600}{360}$$
$$= \frac{60}{36}$$
$$= \frac{10}{6}$$
$$= \frac{5}{3}$$

So the price of the longer trip is $\frac{5}{3}$ that of the shorter trip.

17. (E) If two strips are in the ratio $2 : 3$, it means that one strip is

$$\frac{2}{2+3} = \frac{2}{5}$$

of the total length, and the other strip is

$$\frac{3}{2+3} = \frac{3}{5}$$

of the total length. Assume that x is the total length of the strip. Then one strip is $\frac{2}{5}$ of x, and the other strip is $\frac{3}{5}$ of x. But you know that one strip is longer than the other by 6 inches. That is,

$$\frac{3x}{5} - \frac{2x}{5} = 6$$

Multiplying both sides by 5, you get

$$3x - 2x = 30$$
$$x = 30$$

So the total length of the strip is 30 inches.

18. (D) One method is to try some possible sets of numbers. (Try a few sets to get a "feel" for the validity of a statement.) A possible set of numbers could be

$$2, 4, 6, 8, 10, 12$$

Roman numeral I says that the set has only one number that is divisible by 5. In the set above, this appears to be true, as the only number divisible by 5 is 10.

But if the set is

$$10, 12, 14, 16, 18, 20$$

two numbers are divisible by 5. So roman numeral I is not always true.

Roman numeral II says that the set contains exactly two numbers that are divisible by 3. In the first set above, this appears to be true (6 and 12 are divisible by 3). This is also true in the second set (12 and 18). In fact, this will be true regardless of the set you choose. Even if you choose a set that starts with a multiple of 3, for example,

$$6, 8, 10, 12, 14, 16$$

you see that exactly two numbers are divisible by 3.

Roman numeral III says that the set contains exactly three numbers that are divisible by 4. In the first set above (the one that starts with 2), this appears to be true (4, 8, and 12 are divisible by 4). This is also true in the second set above (the one that starts with 10). In fact, even if the first number in the set is divisible by 4, for example,

$$4, 6, 8, 10, 12, 14$$

there are exactly three numbers that are divisible by 4. So roman numeral III must also be true, which means that II and III must be in the final answer.

19. (D) You know that the area of a parallelogram is

$$\text{area} = \text{base} \times \text{height}$$

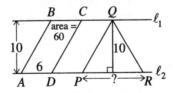

In parallelogram *ABCD*, if you take *AD* as the base $(AD = 6)$, the distance between the two lines (10) can be the height. Then

$$\text{area} = 6 \times 10$$

$$= 60$$

If the area of the parallelogram is 60 and this area is equal to the area of the triangle, then the area of triangle PQR with base PR is also 60. You know that the area of the triangle is

$$\text{area} = \tfrac{1}{2} \times \text{base} \times \text{height}$$

$$60 = \tfrac{1}{2} \times \text{base} \times 10$$

$$120 = \text{base} \times 10$$

$$\frac{120}{10} = \text{base}$$

$$12 = \text{base}$$

20. (A) You know that ##5## designates a circle of area 5. That is,

$$\pi r^2 = \text{area}$$

$$\pi r^2 = 5$$

Then, dividing by π,

$$r^2 = \frac{5}{\pi}$$

and taking the square root leaves

$$r = \sqrt{\frac{5}{\pi}}$$

Then the circumference of the circle is

$$\text{circumference} = 2\pi r$$

and since $r = \sqrt{\dfrac{5}{\pi}}$,

$$\text{circumference} = 2\pi\sqrt{\frac{5}{\pi}}$$

$$= 2\sqrt{\frac{5\pi^2}{\pi}}$$

$$= 2\sqrt{5\pi}$$

21. (D) To find the median income of the nine employees, you first need to arrange the wages in an increasing order:

500, 500, 500, 800, 800, 1,000, 1,000, 1,500, 2,500

The median is the number in the middle, which is 800.

If two of the administrators quit their jobs, the new order is

500, 800, 800, 1,000, 1,000, 1,500, 2,500

and the median is now 1,000.

So the median weekly wage with seven employees as a percent of the wage with all nine employees is

$$\frac{1,000}{800} \times 100 = \frac{10}{8} \times 100$$
$$= \frac{1,000}{8}$$
$$= 125$$

22. (C) If you fold the paper twice and cut a circular hole, there will be four circular holes in the sheet of paper when it is unfolded.

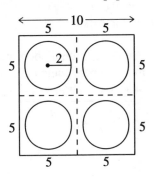

Since the radius of each circle is 2, the area of each circle is

$$\text{area} = \pi r^2$$
$$= \pi (2)^2$$
$$= 4\pi$$

Since there are four such circular holes, the total area of the four circular holes is

$$4 \times 4\pi = 16\pi$$

The area of the sheet of paper is

$$10 \times 10 = 100$$

Therefore, the area of the uncut part of the paper is

uncut area = area of sheet of paper − area of four holes
$$= 100 - 4(4\pi)$$
$$= 100 - 16\pi$$

23. (B) One way to solve this problem is to plug in your own values for the different numbers. You know that $n = 2k$. Since k can be any integer, assume that $k = 2$. Then $n = 2k = 4$. This means that there are four numbers in the set.

You also know that these four numbers are consecutive and even. Then the four numbers could be 2, 4, 6, and 8. Then

$$s = \frac{\text{the sum of all members of the set}}{n}$$
$$= \frac{2+4+6+8}{4}$$
$$= \frac{20}{4}$$
$$= 5$$

Because $s = 5$, you can rule out roman numeral I (which says that s is an even number) and roman numeral III (which says that s is less than n). The only remaining choice is roman numeral II, which means that choice (B) has to be the right answer.

Another way to think about the problem is to realize that because $n = 2k$ (where k is a positive integer), n will always be an even number. Also, notice that s is really the average of all numbers in the set. In other words, s is the average of an even number of consecutive even integers. The average of an even number of consecutive even integers is always odd. Try some of these averages and you'll see.

24. **(B)** At the end of the day of January 1, the ant will be 3 feet above ground. At night, it will have lost 2 feet, so in the morning of January 2, it will be 1 foot above ground. So the ant gains 1 foot per day. Notice that in the morning of January 27, it will be 26 feet above ground. At the end of the day on January 27, it will be $26 + 3 = 29$ feet above ground, and that night it will lose 2 feet so that, in the morning of January 28, it will be 27 feet above ground. However, on January 28 in the daytime, it will gain 3 feet to reach the top.

25. **(A)** If the average of all four numbers in the set is 8, the total of all four numbers is $8 \times 4 = 32$ (because total=average ×number of items). Similarly, if the average of the two smallest numbers is 5, the total of the two smallest numbers must be $5 \times 2 = 10$. If the largest number in the set is 14, you can write

> sum of two smallest numbers
>
> \+ third largest number
>
> \+ largest number
>
> = total of all four numbers

Or

$$10 + \text{third largest number} + 14 = 32$$
$$\text{third largest number} = 32 - 10 - 14$$
$$\text{third largest number} = 8$$

So the set of four numbers can be thought of as

the two smallest numbers, whose total $= 10$
the third largest number $= 8$
the largest number $= 14$

The median of four numbers is the average of the second and the third numbers (because if there are an even number of terms in a set, the median is the average of the two middle numbers). If the third number is 8 and the median is 7, the second number must be 6. If the second number is 6 and the sum of the two smallest numbers is 10, the smallest number must be $10 - 6 = 4$.

Another method, using some reasoning and the answers for help, might be to consider that if the average of the two smallest numbers is 5, then the answer must be either choice (A) 4 or choice (B) 5. Since the total of the four numbers must be 32 to average 8 and the median is 7, the two smallest numbers must be 4 and 6. Using this commonsense approach, you could immediately eliminate choices (C), (D), and (E).